AA/Baedeker
Singapore

Baedeker's

AA

Singapore

THE AUTOMOBILE ASSOCIATION

Imprint

Cover picture: Chinese entrance gate to Tiger Balm Gardens

68 colour photographs
2 general maps, 6 plans, 1 transport plan, 1 city plan

Conception and editorial work:
Redaktionsbüro Harenberg, Schwerte

English Language
Alec Court

Text:
Jürgen Dauth

General direction:
Dr Peter Baumgarten, Stuttgart

Cartography:
Ingenieurbüro für Kartographie Huber & Oberländer, Munich

English translation:
James Hogarth

Source of illustrations:
Dauth, Donath, Rubeli, Tudball (56), Mauritius (1), Storto (3), Uthoff (8), Singapore Tourist Promotion Board

Following the tradition established by Karl Baedeker in 1844, sights of particular interest and hotels of particular quality are distinguished by either one or two asterisks.

To make it easier to locate the various sights listed in the "A to Z" section of the Guide, their coordinates on the city plan are shown in red at the head of each entry.

Only a selection of hotels, restaurants and shopping facilities can be given: no reflection is implied, therefore, on establishments not included.

In a time of rapid change it is difficult to ensure that all the information given is entirely accurate and up to date, and the possibility of error can never be entirely eliminated. Although the publishers can accept no responsibility for inaccuracies and omissions, they are always grateful for corrections and suggestions for improvement.

1st edition

© Baedeker Stuttgart
Original German edition

© 1985 Jarrold and Sons Ltd
English-language edition worldwide

© 1985 The Automobile Association
United Kingdom and Ireland 57176

Licensed user:
Mairs Geographischer Verlag GmbH & Co., Ostfildern-Kemnat bei Stuttgart

Reproductions:
Gölz Repro-Service GmbH, Ludwigsburg

The name *Baedeker* is a registered trademark

Printed in Great Britain by Jarrold and Sons Ltd, Norwich

ISBN 0 86145 323 9

Contents

A reminder:
Singapore attaches great importance to cleanliness, and there are substantial fines (from 50 to 500 dollars) for the dropping of litter (including cigarette ends, paper, etc.). Be careful, therefore, to use the litter bins provided all over the city!

Preface

This Pocket Guide to Singapore is one of the new generation of Baedeker guides.

Baedeker pocket guides, illustrated throughout in colour, are designed to meet the needs of the modern traveller. They are quick and easy to consult, with the principal features of interest described in alphabetical order and practical details about location, opening times, etc., shown in the margin.

Each city guide is divided into three parts. The first part gives a general account of the city, its history, notable personalities and so on; in the second part the principal sights are described; and the third part contains a variety of practical information designed to help visitors to find their way about and make the most of their stay.

The Baedeker pocket guides are noted for their concentration on essentials and their convenience of use. They contain numerous specially drawn plans and coloured illustrations, and in a pocket at the back of the book is a large plan of the city. Each entry in the main part of the guide gives the coordinates of the square on the plan in which the particular feature can be located. Users of this guide, therefore, will have no difficulty in finding what they want to see.

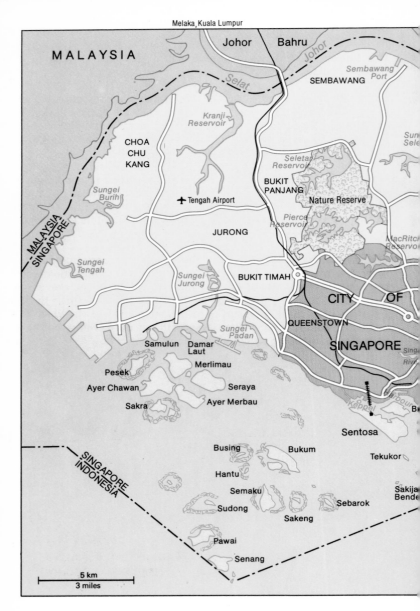

Melaka, Kuala Lumpur

MALAYSIA

Johor Bahru

Selat

Johor

Sembawang Port

SEMBAWANG

Kranji Reservoir

CHOA CHU KANG

Seletar Reservoir

Sungei Selei

Sungei Burih

Tengah Airport

BUKIT PANJANG

Nature Reserve

MALAYSIA SINGAPORE

JURONG

Pierce Reservoir

MacRitchie Reservoir

Sungei Tengah

Sungei Jurong

BUKIT TIMAH

CITY OF

QUEENSTOWN

SINGAPORE

Sungei Padan

Samulun

Damar Laut

Merlimau

Singe River

Pesek

Ayer Chawan

Seraya

Sakra

Ayer Merbau

Keppel

Harbour

B

Sentosa

Busing

Bukum

Tekukor

Hantu

SINGAPORE INDONESIA

Semaku

Sudong

Sakeng

Sebarok

Sakija Bende

Pawai

Senang

5 km
3 miles

8

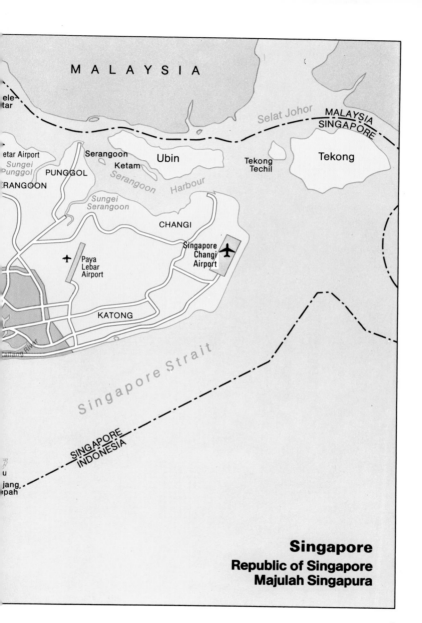

MALAYSIA

ele
tar

Selat Johor   MALAYSIA
SINGAPORE

etar Airport   Serangoon   Ubin   Tekong   Tekong
Sungei   Ketam   Techil
Punggol   PUNGGOL

RANGOON   *Serangoon   Harbour*

Sungei
Serangoon

CHANGI

Singapore
Changi
Airport

+ Paya
   Lebar
   Airport

KATONG

Singapore Strait

SINGAPORE
INDONESIA

u
jang.
pah

Singapore
Republic of Singapore
Majulah Singapura

Facts and Figures

Singapore's
national flag

General

Singapore – officially the Republic of Singapore – is an island state with a total area of 618·1 sq. km (238·6 sq. miles) lying off the southern tip of the Malacca Peninsula (Malaysia) in South-East Asia. It consists of the main island of Singapore (area 548 sq. km (212 sq. miles)) and 54 smaller islands, washed on the west by the Malacca Strait and on the east by the South China Sea. It is linked with the neighbouring state of Malaysia (an elective monarchy) by the Johore Causeway. The Republic of Singapore is a member of the British Commonwealth.

The state

The city of Singapore is capital of the island republic.

Capital

Singapore lies 85 miles north of the Equator in latitude 1°15' N and longitude 103°50' E.

Geographical situation

The national language of Singapore is Malay. In practice, however, this is not much used, the predominant place being taken by English. Mandarin Chinese and Tamil are also recognised as official languages. The business of Parliament is conducted in these four languages, but English and Mandarin are favoured as the languages of business and administration, in order to achieve some degree of homogeneity in this young state with its mix of many peoples. Accordingly from the secondary stage onwards teaching in schools and colleges is permitted in English and Mandarin, but from 1987 only English will be permitted. Parliamentary proceedings and other official records are written only in English.
The Chinese population of Singapore also speaks the Fuchow, Cantonese, Hakka and Hainan dialects of Chinese.
Going about the city, visitors will find street signs, etc., both in English and in Chinese script.

Languages

From the United Kingdom 010 65; from the United States and Canada 011 65.

Telephone dialling code

The total area of the island state is 618·1 sq. km (238·6 sq. miles). While the smaller islands are almost uninhabited, the main island of Singapore has a population of some 2,500,000. Its strict family planning laws have almost entirely prevented the population explosion found elsewhere in Asia, and the annual increase in population is only about 0·16 per cent. The capital, Singapore, occupies about a third of the area of the main island. More than half the population now live in the Government-built satellite towns of Queenstown, Toa Payoh, Kallang, etc. The *kampongs* (villages) around the city are occupied mainly by Malays.

Area and population

The city is not divided into wards in the normal sense, and it has no independent administrative units. The nearest equivalents to local government units are the 79 electoral constituencies with extra-parliamentary Citizen Consultative Committees appointed by the administration.

Civic structure

◀ *Singapore: a city (and a state) of contrasts*

Singapore
and its Neighbours

300 km
187 miles

The Republic of Singapore is a city state, with a President as head of state. The Government consists of the Prime Minister and twelve departmental Ministers, together with a Parliament of 79 Members; it is freely elected by the people of Singapore. The constitution is similar to the British constitution. The President is elected for a four-year term; the period of office of the Cabinet and Parliament is five years. The government is planning a revision of the constitution which will give the President more political power. Henceforth the President is to be elected by the people.
Since Singapore became independent in 1965 the ruling party has been the socialist People's Action Party (PAP).

Government

Administrative authority is exercised directly by the Government.

Administration

Population and Religion

When Sir Thomas Stamford Raffles acquired the island of Singapore for the British East India Company in 1819 it was inhabited only by a handful of Malay fishermen. To promote its development as a commercial centre the Company brought in coolies from South China; under British colonial rule Indians and Ceylonese came to Singapore and in recent years limited numbers of Vietnamese refugees have been admitted. The island state now has a population of over 2,500,000, with a strictly controlled rate of population increase (some 40,000 births annually), since the island's capacity to accommodate any more people is almost exhausted and, as an island, it has no scope for territorial expansion.
Singapore is a multi-racial society, with 76·6 per cent of Chinese, 14·7 per cent Malays, 6·4 per cent Indians, Ceylonese and Pakistanis, and 2·3 per cent Europeans, Jews, Armenians, Arabs and others.

Population

Singapore's ethnic variety is reflected also in its religious diversity. The most important religions are Buddhism, Islam, Hinduism, Christianity and Taoism, but the various ethnic minorities including the Jews and Armenians also practise their faith in their own places of worship. Freedom of religious belief and practice is guaranteed by the constitution. The various denominations are represented on a joint committee, the Interreligious Organisation, which advises the Government on questions of religious harmony. Ecumenical activities in the widest sense, with the participation of all the different religious communities, are taken as a matter of course in Singapore.

Religion

Transport

Singapore's Keppel Harbour lies in a natural inlet on the south coast of the island. It is the world's fourth largest international seaport and the principal centre of trade between Europe and the Far East. It is regularly used by more than 500 international shipping lines, and can accept up to 600 ships at a time including supertankers. In one year the container port can handle 1·2 million containers.
In 1984 the port dealt with a total of 60,500 vessels and some 106 million tonnes of cargo. It has the most modern repair

Port

13

A society in which racial harmony is taken for granted

facilities. The national shipping line is Neptune Orient Lines.

Airport

Singapore's international airport on the Changi Peninsula was opened for traffic in July 1981. The old Paya Lebar Airport, which could handle 3·9 million passengers and 65,000 tonnes of freight annually, was inadequate for future requirements, and is now used for civil traffic only at the busiest times in the year.

Changi Airport is designed to meet Singapore's air traffic requirements into the 21st century; In 1983 8·6 million passengers and 26,000 tonnes of freight were handled and there were 496 regular flights per week. It has two runways, and is so planned that passengers go directly from the aircraft to the terminal building by way of an aerial bridge. The terminal itself can handle a total of 20 million passengers a year. Among the facilities it offers are electronic baggage-handling, several restaurants, large shopping areas for both duty-free goods and travelling requirements, banks and exchange offices, hotel and tourist information, postal services and a baggage storage service. In 1985 a start was made on a new airport building.

The airport is connected with the city by two express highways, and it is planned to introduce rapid mass transport services when required.

Singapore's airport is regularly used by more than 36 international airlines.

Seletar Airport is used by smaller aircraft flying regional services. In 1983 it handled 31,000 passengers and 3144 tonnes of freight.

The national airline is Singapore Airlines (SIA), which possesses the most modern aircraft and flies to 41 cities in 31 different countries. It has direct flights to Auckland, London Heathrow, Los Angeles, Melbourne, Perth, San Francisco and Sydney.

Singapore has no railway system of its own, but has a station linking it with Malayan Railways (Kertapi Tanah Melayu – KTM) by way of the Causeway. There are several express trains daily to the Malaysian capital of Kuala Lumpur, continuing to Butterworth (Penang) and Bangkok (Thailand).

Rail travel

The city and island of Singapore are served by an excellent

Motorways and other roads

Keppel Harbour, Singapore's international seaport

network of roads. The Causeway over the Johore Strait is Singapore's only trunk road.

Buses

Express buses ply daily between Singapore and Kuala Lumpur and Penang in Malaysia. These buses – the Singapore–Johore Express to Kuala Lumpur, the Singapore–Malacca Express and the Singapore–Penang Express – leave from the New Bridge Road car park or the Rochor Centre. There are also municipal bus services within the city.

Mass Rapid Transit

Since 1982 Singapore has been building a Mass Rapid Transit system. This city railway system is to be 67 km (42 miles) long of which 20 km (12 miles) will be underground. There will be an east–west line and a north–south line, intersecting near the City Hall and Raffles Place with 42 stations, to provide better communications between the outer districts and the inner city. The first section will be completed in 1988 between Yio Chu Kang and Clementi through the central business quarter. The whole network is to be operational by 1992.

Trishaws

A distinctive feature of Singapore's traffic is the trishaw, which is a bicycle with a sidecar – similar to a motor-cycle combination, with the motive force provided by muscle-power instead of a motor. These vehicles are becoming increasingly rare in Singapore, but they still exist, and a trip in a trishaw – perhaps through Chinatown – is an experience which visitors should not miss.

Taxis

Singapore has over 11,200 taxis (with meters), which constitute its most important means of transport.

Cableway

Sentosa Island (see under A to Z), off the south coast of Singapore, can be reached from Mount Faber by cableway (aerial cable car).

Culture

General

Singapore's cultural scene shows a mingling of elements in accord with ethnic variety. The individual elements, however, are not combined, but reflect the separateness of the Chinese, Indian and Malay communities. A unified national culture is still in process of emerging. Conditioned as it is by the developing homogenisation based on the English language, it displays strongly Western characteristics. The philosophical heritage of the traditional cultures is intermingled with Western values, with the objective of achieving a national identity which transcends ethnic and community boundaries. The Singapore Cultural Foundation is anxious to arouse and stimulate a national cultural consciousness: no easy matter in a society which thinks mainly in materialistic terms. The Foundation seeks to foster individual artists and promote cultural events and an international cultural exchange.

The modern literature of Singapore has achieved a high standard mainly in poetry. It concerns itself principally with the social conflict between the older immigrant generation and the youth of the present day, with the violent upheavals in a rapidly developing society.

A Singapore trishaw (tricycle + rickshaw) ▶

Universities

In the summer of 1980 the University of Singapore was combined with the Chinese University of Nanyang to form the new National University of Singapore. All teaching is in English; the academic staff is international. The University, together with two institutes of higher technical education, Ngee Ann College and the Singapore Polytechnic, comprised more than 38,000 students in 1985. The standard of university education is comparable with that of the most renowned universities in the West.

The emphasis in academic training lies in the fields of technology and engineering and in the commercial sciences, and increasingly also in what are called the "brain service" disciplines.

Libraries

The National Library of Singapore has more than 1,200,000 titles, of which 650,000 are in English, the rest being in Malay, Chinese, Tamil and other European languages. In addition the Library has a large collection of audio recordings, microfilms and photographs. The whole collection is open to the public. In 1979 the Ministry of Culture began to build up in its Oral History Unit a library of recordings of personal accounts relating to the history of Singapore. Fields already covered are the Singapore pioneers, the political development of Singapore and the Japanese occupation; other subjects are to follow.

The National University of Singapore has one of the largest libraries in South-East Asia, with more than 700,000 books, periodicals, specialist journals and microfilms.

Theatres

The oldest theatre in Singapore is the Victoria Theatre, which was opened in 1862. In 1963 the National Theatre, with seating for 3420, was opened. Both theatres put on productions by visiting companies from the West as well as local productions. Programmes, which are irregular, are announced in the daily Press. The local productions are given by amateur companies. There is also a varied programme of traditional theatre, genuine folk-plays, Indian dance-dramas, Chinese operas and pop events. Other venues for dramatic performances are the People's Theatre in the Kreta Ayer Complex, the auditorium of the Congress Hall, the Cultural Theatre of Singapore, the auditorium of the Development Bank, the Drama Centre and the small theatre in the National Museum.

Symphony Orchestra

Singapore has only one professional orchestra, the Singapore Symphony Orchestra, which receives financial assistance from the Government. It has a strength of 61, just under half of whom are Europeans. It is planned to bring in more musicians born in Singapore who are at present studying at conservatoires abroad. The orchestra puts on a regular programme of concerts: for information consult the daily Press.

Commerce and Industry

A world commercial centre

For 140 years Singapore was the principal British commercial centre on the shipping route between Canton and Calcutta. About the turn of the century it became the marketing centre for natural rubber and tin from Malaysia. Since achieving independence in 1959 it has developed into the most modern industrial, commercial and banking centre in South-East Asia. Its economy is based on foreign investment, which in 1983 accounted for 70 per cent of the total industrial production.

The Singapore Symphony Orchestra, Singapore's only professional orchestra

Leading Japanese, American and European firms use the island republic as their production centre for the Far East and South-East Asia, and it has become the high-tech shop-window for these areas. Preference is given to technology-intensive and export-orientated industries.

Within ASEAN (the Association of South-East Asian Nations), an economic community on the pattern of the EEC which incudes Singapore, Thailand, Malaysia, Indonesia, Brunei and the Philippines, Singapore represents the gateway to world markets. In 1983 its trade amounted to some 106 billion Singapore dollars.

Singapore's principal trading partners are the United States (its largest customer), Malaysia, the European Community and Japan (its largest supplier).

Singapore has one of the largest oil-refineries in the world. The crude oil comes mainly from Saudi Arabia, Kuwait and Iran. Second place is taken by shipbuilding and repair. Singapore's shipyards produce not only ships but also drilling-platforms. Then follow, in terms of value of output, the electrical and electronics industries, engineering, the optical industry and the manufacture of scientific and medical instruments, chemicals, foodstuffs, rubber, textiles and building materials. A petro-chemical complex is being developed on the island of Ayer Merbau. Another major source of revenue is the tourist trade.

Industry

Basically an industrial state, Singapore has some 6500 hectares (16,062 acres) of agricultural land, mainly devoted to stock-farming and supplying almost the whole of the island's requirements of meat.

Agriculture

Notable Personalities

Aw Brothers
(d. 1954 and 1956)

Aw Boon Haw, the "Tiger", and Aw Boon Par, the "Leopard", were two celebrated millionaires and philanthropists who made their name as generous patrons of Chinese culture in Singapore, having made their money from medicinal mixtures based on Chinese herbal medicine. Their best-known product was Tiger Balm, which proved effective in a variety of complaints.

In the Tiger Balm Gardens they left a gigantic monument, with a profusion of colourful sculpture depicting scenes from Chinese mythology and traditional life as well as from modern Singapore.

Joseph Conrad (Józef Teodor Konrad Korzeniowski, 1857–1924)

Joseph, born Józef Teodor Konrad Korzeniowski, was left an orphan and grew up in Russia in the care of relatives; then he went to the School of Seamanship in Marseilles and served in the French and later the British Merchant Navy. He acquired British nationality in 1884, gained his Master's Certificate and sailed the seas of South America and the Far East until 1894. Conrad, who learned English late but wrote his novels and stories in that language, was a masterly delineator of British seafaring life. He lived for several years in Singapore during the second half of the 19th c., gathering material for his novels of life in the East. Singapore and the life of Europeans in the city provided the themes of works such as "Lord Jim", "The End of the Tether" and "The Rescue".

Other works by Conrad were "An Outcast of the Islands" (1896), "The Nigger of the 'Narcissus'" (1897), "Heart of Darkness" (1902), "The Secret Agent" (1907) and "The Rover" (1923).

Datuk Hussein bin Onn
(b. 1922)

Datuk Hussein bin Onn, Prime Minister of Malaysia, was born in Malaysia, trained as a soldier at the Indian Military Academy in Dekra and then studied law in London. In 1942 he enlisted in the Indian Army and served in the Middle East and India during the Second World War; then in 1945 took part in the British campaign which drove the Japanese out of Malaya. Thereafter he spent a year in the public service in Selangor, and in 1946 became head of the youth movement of the United Malays' National Organisation (UMNO), which in the post-war years became the dominant political force in Malaya (later Malaysia). From 1948 to 1957 he was a member of the Parliament of Johore and of its National Council and Executive. From 1960 he practised as a lawyer. In 1968 he rejoined the leadership of UMNO; in 1970 he became a Member of the Parliament and Government of Malaysia, serving as Minister of Education from 1970 to 1973, then as Deputy Premier (1973) and also Minister of Finance; and in 1976, after the sudden death of the Prime Minister, Abdul Razak, he took over as head of the Government.

Lee Kuan Yew (b. 1923)

Lee Kuan Yew, Prime Minister of Singapore, is a pragmatic statesman whose policy is oriented towards the West and who is concerned to create out of the multi-racial population of Singapore a nation of Singaporeans.

Sir Thomas Stamford Raffles, founder of present-day Singapore ▶

Born in Singapore, the son and grandson of wealthy shipowners, he passed out of Raffles College in 1939 and took a law degree at Cambridge in 1946. Thereafter he set up in practice as a lawyer in Singapore (1950). Of his education he once said: "They wanted me to become an educated man, like an Englishman – the very picture of perfection! Like Nehru, I could weep when I think that I speak English better than my mother tongue." He began his political career as adviser to various trade unions (1952), went on to found the left-wing People's Action Party (PAP, 1954) and finally (1959) became Prime Minister of the self-governing state of Singapore. Then, against the will of the Communist opposition, he played a part in the creation of the Federation of Malaysia (1963). Racial differences led in 1965 to Singapore's expulsion from the Federation, and on 9 August in that year Lee Kuan Yew declared the independent Republic of Singapore. In 1968, 1972 and 1976 his party, the PAP, won all the seats in the Parliament of Singapore.

W. Somerset Maugham (1874–1965)

The novelist Somerset Maugham ranks as the best European interpreter of the Malay character.

Born in Paris, Maugham studied medicine in Heidelberg and London but never practised as a doctor. He lived in London, New York and Paris and also spent several years in Singapore and Malaya, where some of his best short stories were written. When living in Singapore he stayed in the Raffles Hotel. His last years were spent on the Côte d'Azur, where he died in 1965.

His principal works were "Of Human Bondage" (1915), "The Moon and Sixpence" (1919), "The Circle" (1921), "The Painted Veil" (1925), "The Razor's Edge" (1944) and "Creatures of Circumstance" (1947).

Sir Thomas Stamford Raffles (1781–1826)

On the evening of 28 January 1819 Sir Thomas Stamford Raffles, Commercial Agent of the British East Indian Company, arrived at the mouth of the Singapore River in the course of a quest for a suitable site for a trading station, and on 6 February he acquired the island of Singapore from Sultan Hussein Mohammed on behalf of the company. Within a few years he had destroyed the hitherto uncontested commercial monopoly of the Dutch, who had colonised the Indonesian island of Java. Raffles introduced Western conceptions of law and democracy into Singapore and founded the University.

H.N. Ridley (1855–1956)

H. N. Ridley, Director of the Singapore Botanic Gardens, planted the first rubber tree in Malaya in 1877, grown from seed smuggled out of Brazil. By the turn of the century rubber production in Singapore and Malaya had overtaken production in South America.

History of Singapore

Since the history of Singapore is inseparable from that of the neighbouring Malay Peninsula (now Malaysia), and since visitors to Singapore can make excursions into Malaysia (see A to Z section), this chronology takes in the development of Malaya as well as Singapore down to the time they became separate states.

Seamen of the Hindu Kingdom of Srivijaya, coming from Sumatra and Java (Indonesia), settle on the Malay Archipelago. Prince Sang Nila Utama founds the kingdom of Temasek ("city on the sea"). According to the legend, he changes its name to Singa Pura ("lion city") after the appearance to him of a lion-like sea creature.

7th–14th c.

The Malay Kingdom of the Majapahit Dynasty, based in Java, conquers the Malay Peninsula and destroys Singapore, which thereafter declines into a small and insignificant fishing village.

1377

Malays from Sumatra create the port of Malacca: a foundation which marks the beginning of the modern history of Malaysia and Singapore. Within a short time Malacca develops into the leading city in South-East Asia.

1398

The Portugese navigator Afonso de Albuquerque takes Malacca.

1511

The Dutch East India Company allies itself with the King of Johore against Malacca.

1606

Malacca passes into Dutch Hands.

1641

Britain takes a lease of the island of Penang.

1786

Britain takes over the Dutch colony of Malacca, but returns it to Holland in 1818.

1795

Singapore is annexed to the Malay sultanate of Johore and becomes the residence of Prince Temenggong. The population consists of a few hundred fishermen.

1811

Sir Thomas Stamford Raffles, agent of the British East India Company, arrives in Singapore and recognises the importance of its natural harbour for the expansion of British trade. He signs a treaty with Prince Temenggong Abdul Rahman for the establishment of a trading station.

6 Feb. 1819

The population of Singapore has grown to 10,000, mainly through the immigration of Chinese coolies.

1822

Sultan Hussein Mohammed Shah cedes the whole of Singapore island to Britain in return for an annual payment of 5000 Spanish dollars. Britain also acquires Malacca from the Dutch in exchange for territory on Sumatra.

1824

Singapore becomes the seat of British administration on the Malacca Strait, subject (along with Penang and Malacca) to the Governor of Bengal.

1867

Although the British colonial authorities had begun to bring in Chinese coolies in the earlier part of the century to build up the new commercial settlement, the great wave of immigration from South China begins in 1874, with annual quotas of several tens of thousands.

1874

Rubber-tree seeds smuggled out of Brazil are planted in Singapore by H. N. Ridley, Director of the Botanic Gardens. With John Dunlop's invention of the pneumatic tyre the rubber tree conquers the Malay Peninsula. Singapore becomes a centre of the trade in natural rubber.

1877

History of Singapore

1895	Establishment of the first federation of the Malay sultanates under British protection.
1915	The sultanate of Johore accepts British protection.
1942	The Japanese General Tomoyaki Yamashita takes the island of Singapore (15 February); capitulation of British forces under General A. E. Percival. The Japanese occupation is followed by a bloody massacre of the Chinese population.
1945	After the Japanese capitulation at the end of the Second World War Singapore returns to British hands (5 September). Singapore and Malaya under British military government.
1948	Young Singapore intellectuals, graduates of British universities, strive for independence from British colonial rule. Singapore becomes a separate Crown colony within the new Federation of Malaya. The first election of a legislative assembly is held on 20 March; a majority of the members are appointed by the British colonial authorities.
1948–60	After the Second World War the Communist Party of Malaya seeks to establish a Communist government in Malaya and Singapore by force of arms. The Communist cadres had gained in strength during the jungle war against the Japanese occupation, in which they had fought alongside British forces. The British colonial authorities declare a state of emergency in Malaya and Singapore. It takes 12 years to quell Communist guerrilla activities.
1954	The 31-year-old lawyer Lee Kuan Yew, a Cambridge graduate, founds the People's Action Party, which aims at full sovereignty for Singapore, in association with an independent Malaysia. Singapore is granted full internal self-government.
1957	Malaya becomes an independent and sovereign member of the Commonwealth (31 August).
1959	After Singapore's first free elections Lee Kuan Yew becomes its first Prime Minister (3 June): a position he still holds.
1963	Foundation of the Federation of Malaysia, with Singapore as a member (16 September). The Malay politician Abdul Rahman remains Prime Minister.
1965	Singapore leaves the Federation of Malaysia (9 August) and becomes an independent republic.
1967	Singapore, Thailand, Malaysia, Indonesia and the Philippines form the Association of South-East Asian Nations (ASEAN). Established in face of the increasing Communist threat in Indochina, the association is originally conceived as an economic community on the model of the EEC, but increasingly develops into a political alliance and military assistance pact.
1971	Dr Benjamin Henry Sheares (non-party) becomes President of the Republic. Lee Kuan Yew's People's Action Party (PAP) wins the 1972 and 1976 parliamentary elections.
1981	President Sheares dies at the age of 72.

The Padang at the turn of the century

Singapore about 1907

Singapore from A to Z

Note

Because of the frequent building activity going on in Singapore some streets are often closed and, therefore, bus services are liable to alteration. In the A to Z section only those bus services are given which start their journeys in the region of Orchard Street or Boulevard and Scotts Road, or which pass these streets, that is the so-called "hotel ring". The choice of buses has been made from the point of view of getting the passenger as near as possible to his or her destination. A direct service is not always possible.

Arab Street D/C4/5

Buses
13, 195

Opening times
Daily 10 a.m.–10 p.m.

This is the shopping centre of the Islamic population of Singapore – the Malays, Arabs, Pakistanis and Muslim Indians. It is a street of little shops in which buyers and sellers haggle over the price. Here visitors will find not only gaudy Asian fabrics but also traditional gold and silver jewellery. The goldsmiths will make pieces to order and to any desired design. Arab Street is most conveniently reached from Beach Road. At the intersection with North Bridge Road is the Sultan Mosque (see entry).

The Armenian Apostolic Church, Singapore's oldest Christian church

Armenian Apostolic Church of St Gregory

C4

The Church of St Gregory the Illuminator, built in 1835 by Armenian refugees from Turkey, is Singapore's oldest Christian church. It is no longer used for worship but is protected as a national monument. It stands at the foot of the oldest Christian cemetery in Singapore, on Fort Canning Rise, also known as the Forbidden Hill. The church can be seen in the course of the History on Foot walk organised by the Singapore Tourist Promotion Board (see under Practical Information).

The Armenian population of Singapore now amounts to no more than about 60 people.

In the same street is the Chinese Chamber of Commerce (see entry).

Location
Hill Street

Buses
124, 173, 174

Conducted tours
History on Foot

Bird Park

See Jurong Town

*Botanic Gardens

B1

The Botanic Gardens, laid out by the British authorities in 1859 for research purposes, are among the most beautiful tropical gardens in the world, with more than half a million tropical plants. A pavilion in Victorian style houses the largest herbarium in Asia.

Location
Cluny Road/Holland Road

Buses
7, 14, 95, 106, 112, 174, 188

The Botanic Gardens – one of the most beautiful tropical gardens in the world

Bukit Timah Nature Reserve *Central Park*

Opening times
Daily 5 a.m.–10 p.m.

In 1877 the British Director of the Botanic Gardens, H. N. Ridley, planted the first rubber trees in Malaysia here on an experimental basis. The experiment was successful, and by the turn of the century natural rubber had become the most important commercial product of Singapore and Malaysia.

The gardens cover an area of 32 hectares (80 acres). A particularly striking feature is a jungle-like area, with huge trees, lianas as thick as a man's arm, giant ferns and a profusion of tropical flowers, which gives an authentic picture of Singapore's original natural vegetation.

Equally impressive is the Orchid Pavilion, in which the various stages in the development of orchids, from seed to blossom, are displayed in glass vessels. There is also a beautiful lake decked with water-lilies and inhabited by black swans. A good two hours should be allowed for seeing the gardens.

Bukit Timah Nature Reserve

Location
Bukit Timah Road

Buses
5, 170, 171, 172, 173, 177, 180, 181, 182, 200

Distance
12 km (7½ miles) – 30 minutes' drive

Bukit Timah is the largest of Singapore's nature reserves, with an area of 75 hectares (185 acres), and also the most unspoiled (cars prohibited). Here well-maintained footpaths, with rest huts at intervals, run through primeval jungle. The tigers which formerly inhabited Singapore's forests are no longer to be found, but there are still large families of monkeys.

The road to the Bukit Timah Nature Reserve passes a number of smaller parks – Binjai Park, Hongkong Park, Leedon Park, Eden Park and Berzay Park.

Central Park

This large park of some 40 hectares (100 acres) is a cultural complex as well as a park. In it are an historic old cemetery, the National Theatre, the National Museum (see entry), the Van Kleef Aquarium (see entry), the Cultural Centre and, near by, the beautiful River Valley Swimming Pool.
From the high ground of Central Park there are fine views of the whole city of Singapore.
Opening times are daily until 11 p.m.

Location
Clemenceau Avenue

Buses
12, 122, 123, 139, 143, 148, 164, 168, 180, 195

Change Alley D4

This famous little shopping lane is more than a street of shops: it is an ethnic melting-pot. In this swarming crowd of humanity are found representatives of every race in Asia, buying and selling, bargaining, so long as daylight lasts – though little enough daylight penetrates at any time into this narrow lane, this forest of neon signs, which the passer-by might miss completely were it not for the name in neon letters over the concealed entrance on Collyer Quay. Change Alley is an Asian bazaar offering an extraordinary range of goods, from curios and antiques to the most modern optical and electronic appliances. Fixed prices are unknown here: bargaining is the main pleasure of doing business. And if you are in need of money, there are the Muslim Indian money-changers who take the place of banks here and have given Change Alley its name.

Location
Collyer Quay

Buses
1, 8, 10, 15, 20, 30, 50, 60, 70, 75, 80, 82, 94, 97, 100, 107, 112, 125, 138, 141, 146, 189

Opening times
Daily 10 a.m.–10 p.m.

Changi Beach

The road to this beautiful bathing beach runs through the Singapore countryside, past typical Malay villages (*kampongs*) which have preserved something of the life of the older Singapore, a sleepy island inhabited only by fishermen.
The sandy beach is washed by the South China Sea, and offers facilities for every conceivable kind of water sport. Scuba enthusiasts should contact the Singapore Sub-Aqua Club, tel. 445 6253.

Location
Upper Changi Road

Buses
13; change to 1 or 2 at Victoria Street

Distance
30 minutes' drive E of the city

**Chettiar Temple C3

The original Chettiar Temple, dedicated to the Hindu god Subramaniam (also known as Muruga or Sri Dhanadayhapani), the Preserver, was built between 1855 and 1860 in the style of South India. The old building has been demolished and replaced by a new one designed in the original style.
The Chettiars were a South Indian caste, originally from the Madras area, who were brought to Singapore by the British. They are a dark-skinned Tamil race, and traditionally follow the trades of money-changers and money-lenders.
The temple is noted for the macabre Thaipusam festival, a Hindu festival of penance and thanksgiving celebrated at the end of January or the beginning of February (varying according to the lunar calendar). The worshippers carry, in honour of Subramaniam, a miniature temple known as the

Location
Tank Road

Buses
123, 143

Chettiars Hindu Temple

kavadi which may weigh anything up to half a hundredweight. While in a trance they pierce their cheeks and tongue with spikes and spears up to 10 feet long and carry lemons suspended from their skin on silver hooks. In October the temple is the scene of a more joyous celebration, the festival of Navarathri or the Nine Nights, which is accompanied by classical dances and traditional music; on the 10th day a silver horse is paraded through the streets.

Chinatown D/E3/4

Here, within an area of little more than 2 sq. km (¾ sq. mile), live some 75,000 people, their houses closely packed together in narrow lanes and alleys. Singapore's Chinatown is a carry-over from the time when a three-storey building anywhere in the town was regarded as a skyscraper. Architecturally it is a mixture of traditional Chinese building and the British colonial style, to which Chinatown owes its colonnades. Later, well-to-do Chinese visiting Europe brought back classical features with them. The resultant stylistic conglomerate is known as Chinese Baroque. Chinatown ends at the Singapore River, where the modern world begins.

Old traditions are slow to die; and this is no less true of the rhythm of life in Chinatown and the old crafts still practised there. The candle-makers are to be found in China Street, with small noodle factories close by; joss sticks are made in Peking

Location
Around South Bridge and New Bridge Road area

Buses
124, 143, 173, 174

◄ *Change Alley – shopping street and ethnic melting-pot*

Chinatown

Street; the figures of gods for Chinese temples are carved in Club Street. The tailors of Chinatown will make shirts, suits and other items of clothing at a day's notice.

Any Chinese resident of Singapore who did not have enough room to die with the traditional pomp and ceremony of a Chinese funeral, could, until a short time ago, hire one of the "death houses" in Sago Lane for his last hours. The death houses, however, had to give way to civic development. Certainly one still comes across Chinese soothsayers, although their trade is prohibited in Singapore.

The once-famous street markets of Chinatown as well as the street kitchens have been moved to the newly built Kreta Ayer Complex in Sago Lane. Here both the morning markets and the night market (see Night Markets) are held.

For the benefit of the more apprehensive visitor it should be said that the food served in the street kitchens will not disagree with a Western stomach.

Chinese Chamber of Commerce   C4

Location
Hill Street

Buses
124, 173, 174

The Chinese Chamber of Commerce occupies a tall modern building which incorporates traditional Chinese architectural elements.

Note, in particular, the pagoda-style double curving roof, the very fine mosaics on the surrounding walls, modelled on those in the Imperial Palace in Peking, and the richly ornamented red main doorway in traditional Chinese palace style.

Orchard Road

Bras Basah Road

Reuben Mannaseh Meyer Synagogue

A.A. House

River Valley Road

Church of Sacred Heart

Cathedral of the Good Shepherd

Odeon Theatre

Shaw Towers

Fort Canning

Chettiars Hindu Temple

Central Park

Fort Canning Reservoir

National Library

American Church

Convent of the Holy Infant Jesus

Raffles Hotel

National Theatre

Van Kleef Aquarium

Masonic Hall

St. Andrew's Cathedral

War Memorial Park

Singapore River

Colombo Court

City Hall

Esplanade Restaurant

Ganges Avenue

Market

Tan Si Chong Su Temple

Melaka Mosque

Supreme Court

Parliament

Cenotaph

Lim Bo Seng Memorial

Market

Tong Chai Building

12

Hong Lim Centre

Government Offices

Victoria Hall & Theatre

Merlion

Pearl's Hill Reservoir

Majestic Theatre

People's Park Center

Wak Hai Cheng Bio

Collyer Quay

Clifford Pier

People's Park Complex

Jamae Mosque

Oriental Theatre

Fuk Tak Ch'i

Ocean Building

Yangtze Theatre

Outram Road

Hindu Temple

13

Sri Mariamman Temple

14

Street

Denmark House

16

Singapore General Hospital

Maxwell Market

15

Al-Abrar Mosque

Hong Leong Building

University

Nell

Metropole Theatre

Cecil Street

Robinson Road

P.S.A. Gate 6

Reclaimed Land

Shipping Office

Market

Chinese Temple

Market

Conference Hall

P.S.A. Gate 5

Yan Kit Swimming Pool

International Plaza

Spottiswoode Park

Railway Station

Anson Road

Tua Pekong Temple

Finger Pier

Keppel Road

P.S.A. Gate 2

Tanjong Pagar Complex

Neptune Building

National Maritime Board Building

Empire Dock

Container Port Building

P.S.A. Gate 4

Passenger Terminal

P.S.A. Gate 3

Main Wharf

Victoria Dock

East Wharf Road

Albert Dock

Container Port

Keppel

Harbour

Chinatown

250 m
275 yds

East Lagoon

East Lagoon

Sentosa Island

1 Presbyterian Church
2 St. Joseph's Institution
3 Clyde Terrace Market
4 Cultural Centre
5 National Museum & Art Gallery
6 Bethesda Church
7 Capitol Theatre
8 Chinese Chamber of Commerce
9 Singapore Recreation Club
10 Keramat Iskandar Shah
11 Singapore Cricket Club
12 Ministry of Labour
13 Kreta Ayer People's Theatre
14 Nagaar Durga Shrine
15 Thian Hok Keng
16 Overseas Union Shopping Centre

Chinese Opera

Information
Tourist Information
tel. 235 6611

There are regular performances of Chinese operas in Singapore, usually given in the street. The companies have no permanent headquarters.

The Chinese opera (*wayang*) is a traditional art brought to Singapore by incomers from the Chinese mainland. It usually depicts scenes from life at the Imperial Court and heroic legends. The themes are predominantly tragic and romantic.

For times and places of performances, ask Tourist Information, tel. 235 6611.

Clifford Pier

See Keppel Harbour

Crocodile Farm

Location
Upper Serangoon Road

Bus
111

Opening times
8.30 a.m.–5 p.m.

In the crocodile farm on Upper Serangoon Road some hundreds of crocodiles, alligators, lizards and snakes are bred for Singapore's leatherworking industry.

Most of the skins, after tanning and polishing, are sold to leatherworking firms, but some of them are used on the farm for the manufacture of souvenirs (Singapore being renowned for its high-quality crocodile-skin products) for sale to visitors.

East Coast Lagoon

Location
East Coast Parkway

Buses
16; alight at Marine Parade
Terminal

Opening times
Mon.–Sat. 9 a.m.–6.30 p.m.;
Sun. 8 a.m.–6.30 p.m.

This artificial lagoon must surely be the largest swimming-pool in the world: it is the equivalent of 40 indoor pools and can accommodate 6000 bathers at the same time. It is supplied with water by the South China Sea, but the waves are machine-made. There are 17 m (56 ft) high chutes down which bathers can hurtle into the swirling waters of the pool.

Here, too, there are picnic areas, street-kitchens and changing-rooms, as well as tennis-courts (tel. 442 5966). In the East Coast Recreation Centre there are 17 squash courts and in the nearby Parkland Driving Range (tel. 440 6726/348 5609) there is an 18-hole golf-course.

Elizabeth Walk   D4

Location
Connaught Drive

Buses
1, 8, 10, 15, 20, 30, 50, 60,
70, 75, 80, 82, 94, 97, 100,
107, 112, 125, 138, 141,
146, 189

Named after Queen Elizabeth II and officially called Queen Elizabeth Walk, this was formerly known as the Promenade.

This seafront promenade, with a fine view of the harbour, runs from the Satay Club (Malay street-kitchens) to Merlion Park, passing in front of City Hall. It is screened by gardens from the busy traffic of Connaught Drive. During the colonial period it was a favourite place of resort for the social élite of the colony; it is now the domain of the younger generation.

Here Stamford Raffles set foot on the soil of Singapore for the

A traditional Chinese opera

Crocodiles – raw material for the leatherwork industry

In the Empress Place Park

first time; there is a monument to him near here, on the Padang. The small fountain in Elizabeth Walk commemorates the Chinese philanthropist Tan Kim Seng, who financed Chinatown's first water-supply. Another monument, popularly known as the Four Chopsticks, commemorates the Resistance leader Lim Bo Seng, who was tortured to death during the Second World War but died with his lips sealed.

Emerald Hill   B/C3

Location
Junction of Emerald Hill
Road and Orchard Road

Buses
7, 13, 14, 16, 23, 64, 65, 92,
95, 106, 111, 123, 124, 132,
132A, 139, 140, 143, 168,
171, 173, CBD 1

The Emerald Hill district, and in particular the old buildings in the area, are protected as national monuments. Here, as in Chinatown (see entry), the predominant style is Chinese Baroque, a mingling of traditional Chinese elements and the British colonial style. Later this colourful architecture was still further enriched with features taken from European Renaissance and Baroque, producing an architectural style found only in Chinese colonial territories.

Empress Place (Park)   D4

Location
High Street/Boat Quay

This landscaped park was laid out in 1972 on a site which had previously been a car park. Here, after the last war, was re-erected the statue of Sir Stamford Raffles, founder of modern Singapore, which had been pulled down by the Japanese. On the marble base on which the bronze statue stands are inscriptions in the four principal languages of Singapore (Malay, Chinese, Tamil and English) recording the foundation of the town.

Empress Place, named after Queen Victoria, lies below the Victoria Memorial Hall, now the Victoria Theatre.

Buses
1, 8, 10, 15, 20, 30, 50, 60, 70, 75, 80, 82, 94, 97, 100, 107, 112, 125, 138, 141, 146, 189

Fort Canning Rise (Tomb of Sultan Iskandar Shah)   C3

Fort Canning Rise was formerly known as Bukit Larangan, the Forbidden Hill. Tradition has it that Sultan Iskandar Shah, last Malay ruler of Singapore, was buried on the hill after the destruction of his kingdom in 1391 by the Majapahites (a Sumatran ruling family). His tomb is venerated by the Muslim Malays as a *keramat* (holy place).

This was the site of ancient Singapura. Recent excavations have brought to light gold ornaments and pottery of an early Malay settlement. The finds are exhibited in the National Museum.

Location
Coleman Street

Buses
7, 13, 14, 16, CBD 1; as far as Bras Basah Road

Hajjah Fatima Mosque   B5

Dating from about 1845, this charming little mosque was built by a Malay lady in token of her love for a nobleman of the Bugis community.

Location Beach Road

Bus 13 to Kallang Road

The Hajjah Fatima Mosque

37

A craftsman at work in the Handicraft Centre

Handicraft Centre   B1

Location
Tanglin Road

Buses
7, 13, 14, 23, 64, 95, 106,
111, 132, 174, 390

Opening times
Daily 10 a.m.–8 p.m.

The Handicraft Centre, near Tudor Court, offers the largest assortment of the arts and crafts of Singapore, together with a variety of products from other Asian countries, particularly Malaysia, Indonesia and India. The goods it displays are specially designed to appeal to tourists. In many of the establishments visitors can not only buy the articles but see them being made. Particularly attractive buys are Persian carpets, batik-work from Indonesia, masks from Java and Bali, silk from India and rosewood and ivory carving.

Harbour

See Keppel Harbour

High Street   D4

Buses
124, 173, 174

Opening times
Daily 10 a.m.–10 p.m.

With more than 40 large stores and several hundred smaller shops, the High Street is one of Singapore's busiest shopping streets. Here are offered for sale optical and electronic appliances made by the world's best-known manufacturers, and watches and jewellery by the most celebrated designers. The fabrics displayed range from Chinese silk to Irish linen. Some of the best shops for jade, pearls and traditional jewellery are to be found here.

*House of Jade   B1

The House of Jade is the former residence of the families of Aw Boon Haw (the"Tiger") and Aw Boon Par (the "Leopard"), who made millions from the sale of their Tiger Balm, a medicament made from ethereal oils (see Introduction – Notable Personalities and A to Z – Tiger Balm Garden). The two brothers assembled the finest ever private collection of Chinese jade, including pieces dating from the Ching Dynasty (1644–1911) and the Sung Dynasty (960–1279). The collection of jade and some valuable Chinese engravings and water-colours were bequeathed to the State and are now in the National Museum (see entry).
The building itself is interesting for its colonial architecture.

Location
Tanglin Road/Nassim Road

Buses
7, 13, 14, 23, 64, 95, 106, 111, 132, 174, 390

**Johor Bahru (Johore Baharu; Malaysia)

Johor Bahru is capital of the Malaysian sultanate of Johore, the seat of government and royal residence of the Sultan of Johore. It lies on the north side of Johore Strait (Selat Johor) on the Malaysian mainland, linked with Singapore by the 1 km (¾ mile) long Causeway.
The town (founded by Sultan Abu Bakar in 1855) and surrounding area contain many relics and reminiscences of Malaysian history. Visitors contemplating a trip to Johor Bahru can obtain information from the Tourist Development Corporation Malaysia, Singapore; tel. 532 6321 6351.

Location
Malaysia

Buses
Singapore–Johore Express, Rocher Centre, Bencoolen Street

Distance
25 km (15 miles) N

Abu Bakar Mosque

This royal mosque, built in 1892 by Sultan Abu Bakar, stands on Jalan Abu Bakar, a street running parallel to the Johore Strait. Its architecture shows a mingling of the Moorish with the British colonial style. The combination is remarkably successful, making this one of the finest mosques in Malaysia. Visitors are admitted outside the hours of prayer.

Location
Jalan Abu Bakar

Open
Outside times of prayer

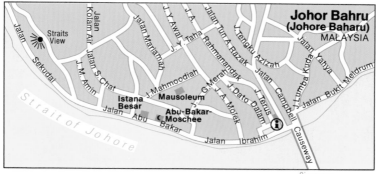

Singapore

39

The Istana Besar, Johor Bahru

The Japanese tea-house, Istana Garden, Johor Bahru

Istana Besar

The ceremonial palace of the Sultan of Johore, the Istana Besar, also situated on the Jalan Abu Bakar, was built in 1866 as the first residence of the royal family. The palace is now used only for official functions (receptions, coronations and various royal ceremonies); the Sultan lives in a new palace, the Istana Bukit Serene, which is not open to the public.

Like the Abu Bakar Mosque, the Istana Besar is built in a style which mingles Moorish and British colonial features, and is decorated with traditional Malaysian carving. In the north wing is the throne room, and adjoining this is a small museum displaying Court dress, the royal insignia, weapons and hunting trophies.

The palace can be seen on weekdays between 9 a.m. and midday with a permit from the Johore tourist authorities.

Location
Jalan Abu Bakar

Opening times
Palace: Mon.–Sat.
9 a.m.–midday (with permit).
Gardens: daily, all day

Istana Garden

The palace gardens, which are open to the public throughout the day, are among the most beautiful in Malaysia. Particularly fine are the orchid garden and the fern garden. There is also a Japanese garden with a Japanese tea-house, created in honour of a visit by the Crown Prince of Japan in 1936.

Royal Mausoleum

This has been the burial-place of the royal family of Johore since the foundation of the town.

The Mausoleum itself, in a style modelled on Arab architecture, is not open to the public, but there are many other interesting Muslim tombs in the cemetery.

Location
Jalan Mahmoodiah

*Jurong Town

Jurong is Singapore's most modern industrial zone, almost an independent town. Here, in a garden-like setting on land reclaimed from swamp, some 2260 firms have established themselves. The petrochemicals industry is a predominant element, and Jurong has one of the largest refineries in the world.

Jurong is 30 minutes' drive from the city centre

Buses
7, 13, 14, 16, 23, 64, 65, 92,
106, 111, 124, 140, 168,
171, 173, 174, 390 to
MacDonald House, Orchard
Yaohan, on foot to Penang
Road, bus 198 to Jurong.
From Jurong change to 242,
406 to Chinese Garden, 250
to Bird Park.

Chinese Garden

The Chinese Garden of Jurong covers an area of over 13 hectares (35 acres), with a network of footpaths providing easy access to its beauties. Entered by an imposing gateway, the garden contains several pagodas, a stone boat, a nine-arched bridge and a Chinese tea-house. The architecture, in a style modelled on that of the Sung Dynasty (960–1279), is reminiscent of the Summer Palace in Peking.
Opening times are daily 9 a.m.–6 p.m.

Location
Near Yuan Ching Road

Entrance
Ask for a combined ticket for
Chinese and Japanese
Gardens

Chinese Garden, Jurong

Japanese Garden

Opening times
Mon.–Sat. 9 a.m.–6 p.m.;
Sun. and pub. holidays
8.30 a.m.–6 p.m.

The Seiwaen Japanese Garden of Juruno presents over 32 acres of typical Japanese garden layout, with stone gardens, goldfish ponds, Lotus ponds, stone lanterns and little Pagodas.

Bird Park

Opening times
Mon.–Fri. 9 a.m.–6 p.m.
Sat., Sun. and pub. holidays
9 a.m.–7 p.m.

Jurong Bird Park, established in 1971, occupies an area of 20 hectares (50 acres) on the hill of Bukit Peropok, in the centre of the town. It contains over 3500 birds from all over the world, including flamingoes, birds of paradise, emus and rare tropical birds. There is also a 2 hectare (5 acre) "flight garden" in which the birds live in surroundings resembling their natural habitat.

Visitors are free to walk about the park, or they can take a trip round it on a miniature railway. The route runs past an artificial waterfall which plunges over a granite crag 30 m (100 ft) high into an artificial river.

The ponds, lakes and lagoons in the park are the haunt of every species of waterfowl, and there is even a penguin-pool – the park's most popular attraction – in which, with the help of supplies of ice, the penguins (not otherwise found in the tropics) are made to feel at home. Daily presentation 10.30 a.m.

Kelongs

The kelongs of Singapore are a traditional type of fish-trap, used by the Malays for many hundreds of years. Long bamboo poles are driven into the sea bottom at points where it is relatively shallow, and on these is constructed a platform bearing a small hut. Some of the larger kelongs are like miniature villages.

The kelongs are to be found around the offshore islands but are no longer included in the excursion programme organised by the Tourist Promotion Board. Anyone interested in a visit to a kelong should seek the help of the proprietor of one of the seafood restaurants in Ponggol or Tuas, which are normally supplied by the kelongs. Boats will usually be made available when a seafood meal is ordered beforehand.

Location
Southern Islands

Buses
To Ponggol 64, 65, 106, 111
To Serangoon Road 83, 84
To Tuas 174 as far as Jurong
Crescent change to 175

Keppel Harbour   F/G1–3

Keppel Harbour, one of the world's largest international seaports, occupies a natural inlet at the southernmost point of Singapore. It can accept up to 600 vessels at the same time, and in 1983 handled over 106 million tonnes of freight.

Clifford Pier is the oldest part of the port installations, and is still the main mooring-place for overseas ships.

Here can be seen ocean-going ships from all over the world, tankers and freighters, together with hundreds of Chinese junks, barges, sampans, fishing-boats and sailing-boats. Of

Buses
CBD 1, 8, 10, 15, 20, 30, 50, 60, 70, 80, 82, 94, 97, 100, 107, 112, 125, 130, 131, 141, 146, 161, 163, 172, 175, 189

Boats
Clifford Pier

Singapore River: Sampans

Keppel Harbour in the early morning

Information
Tourist information offices
and travel agencies

particular interest are the supertankers, and the junks which operate within the harbour as lighters.

Near by are the offices of the port administration.

Clifford Pier is also the departure point for harbour and island cruises. The harbour cruise goes round the various wharves and also takes in the container port.

Other cruises visit Malay villages and various smaller islands lying off the main island of Singapore. Information and booking: see Practical Information (Information, Boat trips).

Kota Tinggi (Malaysia)

Location
Malaysia; on road from
Johor Bahru to Mersing

Buses
See Practical Information –
Bus Trips

Kota Tinggi is a small town in the sultanate of Johore. The road from Johor Bahru (see entry), capital of the sultanate, passes by large pineapple plantations. Johore's pineapples, reputed to be the sweetest in the world, are grown for canning and export.

Kota Tinggi's main sights are its falls and its recreation park. It is 85 km (53 miles) north of Singapore.

Kota Tinggi Falls

Kota Tinggi Falls, 9 km (6 miles) east of the town, tumble from a height of 35 m (115 ft) into a natural basin.

Gunong Muntahak Park

The area around the falls has been developed as a recreation area, with picnic and bathing places. Overnight accommodation is available in a modest cottage hotel. The hill of Gunong Muntahak (624 m (2047 ft)) offers scope for adventurous jungle walks.

Near Kota Tinggi Falls

Kranji War Memorial

Round Kranji War Memorial are buried the 24,000 men and women who lost their lives during the Second World War in resisting the Japanese invasion and occupation. The memorial, a 25 m (80 ft) high mast topped by a golden star, bears the inscription "They died for all free men" in six languages (Chinese, English, Malay, Tamil, Urdu and Gurkhali).

Location
Mandai Road/Woodlands Road

Buses
170, 178, 180, 181, 182, 208

*Kuan Yin Temple   C4

This Taoist temple, dedicated to the goddess of mercy, is one of the most popular Chinese temples in Singapore. Here, appealing to the goddess Kuan Yin, the Chinese seek peace and protection from the adversities of life.
The statue of the goddess in the main hall of the temple is clad in many layers of silk, votive offerings from grateful worshippers. The temple is the scene of busy ritual activity.

Location
Waterloo Street

Buses
7, 13, 14, 16, CBD 1

Kusu Island

Kusu is one of the 54 smaller island which surround the main island of Singapore. It lies 7 km (4½ miles) south of Singapore.

Buses
143 as far as World Trade Centre

Little India

In the Kuan Yin Temple

Kusu Island Temple (Tua Pek Kong)

Boats
From World Trade Centre
(ferry) Mon–Sat 10 a.m.,
1.30 p.m.; Sun and pub.
holidays 9, 10, and
11.20 a.m., 12.20, 1.40,
2.40, 4, 5, and 7.20 p.m.;
Return 1 hour after departure
from W.T.C.

The principal feature of interest on the island is a Taoist temple dedicated to Tua Pek Kong, the Chinese god of fortune. The delicately ornamented curving pagoda roofs are supported on columns, some of which stand on the rocky sea-bottom. The best time to visit the temple is at the end of October and beginning of November, when the Kusu Festival is celebrated and large numbers of gaily decorated sampans moor at the temple. The festival lasts a month, and during this period the god shows himself liberal in granting prosperity to those who pay him respect.

*Little India   B4

Location
Serangoon Road

Buses
23, 64, 65, 106, 111, 198

The Indian quarter of Singapore, known as Little India, is centred on Serangoon Road. A visitor to this part of the city, surrounded by men in *dhotis* (loincloths) and women in colourful saris, could be excused for believing himself suddenly transported to India.

The shops in this quarter sell spices, herbs and other foodstuffs from India, Indian arts and crafts, silk and muslin, brocades and cotton.

Small Hindu temples lie hidden in side streets, and the noise and chatter of the streets and markets, which are far from muted, are drowned by the sound of choral singing, classical dance or temple music, or hit tunes from Hindi films.

MacRitchie Reservoir

The MacRitchie Reservoir holds 315,000,000 litres (70,000,000 gallons) of rainwater. The surrounding area has been laid out as a park, with many attractive footpaths. Concerts are occasionally given in the pavilion above the reservoir, and there is a floating fountain which constantly changes its form and is illuminated after dark to produce an enchanting pattern of light and water.

Location
Lornie Road

Buses
104, 132, 132A

* * Malacca (Melaka; Malaysia)

Although Malacca is 250 km (155 miles) from Singapore, it is well worth taking a two-day trip there if time permits, for Malacca makes a rewarding complement to a stay in Singapore.

Malacca is capital of the state of the same name in the Federation of Malaysia – one of the four states ruled not by a Sultan but by a Governor.

The town, situated at the mouth of the Malacca River, was founded by Sultan Iskandar Shah in the 13th c., and was the capital of the first Malay kingdom, which by about 1400 was exchanging Ambassadors with China. The King reigning at that time in Malacca was Parameswara, ruler of the Hindu-Malay kingdom, which had moved its capital from Singapore to Malacca. Parameswara married a Chinese Princess, and this alliance made the town, with its natural harbour, the

Location
Malaysia

Buses
Singapore–Malacca Express
New Bridge Road car park
tel: 223 8868

Distance
250 km (155 miles) N

Information
Malacca Tourist Centre,
Jalan Laksamana or: Tourist
Development Corporation
Malaysia, Singapore
tel: 532 6321

Santiago Gate, Malacca

Tranquera Mosque, Malacca

commercial centre of South-East Asia, dealing mainly in condiments and spices. Islam was brought to Malacca by Arab traders, and from there spread all over the Malay Peninsula. In 1511 the Portuguese captured the town and the Malay ruler fled to Johore. The Portuguese admiral, Albuquerque, encouraged mixed marriages between his troops and Malay girls, and the descendants of these unions still live in the Portuguese village of Malacca and speak a medieval form of Portuguese. In 1614 the town was taken by the Dutch, who 150 years later ceded it to Britain in exchange for British-held territories on Sumatra.

Malacca is a focal point of Malaysian history. The different periods of that history and the various rulers who have held sway here have left their mark in the form of historic old buildings, some of them still excellently preserved. Malacca's past is also reflected in a lively trade in antiques.

Malacca has now lost its importance as the commercial centre of South-East Asia, a role taken over by Singapore; and its harbour, of which a Portuguese seaman once wrote, "Malacca is the richest seaport in the world, with the largest number of traders and of ships", is now largely silted up.

Bukit China (Chinese Cemetery)

Location
Jalan Bukit China

This hill on Jalan Bukit China, the street named after it, is occupied by the largest Chinese cemetery outside China. Some

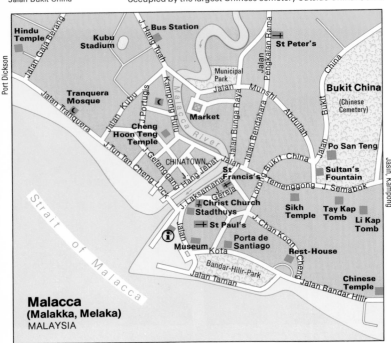

Malacca
(Malakka, Melaka)
MALAYSIA

Chinese tombs in the Bukit China Cemetery, Malacca

of the tombs date back to about 1400. Of the palace of the Chinese princess Hong Lim Poh, who became the wife of King Parameswara and lived here with 500 maids-in-waiting, there remain only a few foundations.

Cheng Hoon Teng Temple

This Taoist temple is the oldest and most lavishly decorated Chinese temple in Malaysia. Built in 1704 by a wealthy merchant named Chan Ki Lock, it is dedicated to the Chinese admiral Cheng Ho, Peking's special envoy at the Court of Malacca, who later achieved divine status.

Among its most striking features are the pagoda roofs, decorated with glazed filigree reliefs depicting scenes from Chinese myths. In the main hall is an altar with lacquer-painting of the utmost delicacy on the front. In the side halls are stelae representing the dead, which in Taoist belief are visited from time to time by the souls of the ancestors so that they may be supplied with food by their descendants.

Location
Temple Street

Chinatown

In this quarter around the Malacca River there are still many houses dating back for more than 200 years, some of them ancestral family homes notable for their magnificence. There are the finest examples of the style known as Chinese Baroque, a mingling of Chinese features, colonial influences and classical-style borrowings from Europe.

49

Exterior of the Cheng Hoon Teng Temple, Malacca . . .

. . . and the interior

In this area, too, particularly in Jalan Hang Jebat (formerly Jonker Street) are Malacca's antique shops, tempting the buyer with furniture, domestic equipment, traditional jewellery and fine porcelain, and offering an epitome of the town's history.

Best view of the area is from the third storey of the former Borneo Company building on the corner of Jalan Tan Cheng Lock and Lorong Hang Jebat.

Christ Church

This Anglican church was originally built by the Dutch in 1753, using red bricks brought by sea from Holland. The walls were later given a facing of red laterite.

Note in particular the roof beams, each sawn from a single log, and the old tombstones, with inscriptions redolent of Dutch history. The silver Communion vessels still bear the Dutch coat of arms.

Location
Jalan Laksamana

St Paul's Church

St Paul's Church is now a ruin, though the outer walls have been restored. The church, on Residency Hill, was founded in 1521 by the Portuguese Governor, Albuquerque, and was the episcopal church of St Francis Xavier, Bishop of the Portuguese possessions. It passed into the hands of the Dutch in 1753.

There are a number of old tombstones in the ruins.

Location
Jalan Kota

Santiago Gate (Porta de Santiago)

The only relic of the Portuguese fortifications of Malacca is the Porta de Santiago, the town's south gate, built by Albuquerque. It was destroyed by the British in 1807.

The ruins have been restored, and there are some well-preserved reliefs.

Location
Jalan Kota

Stadthuys

The old Town Hall, built in stages between 1641 and 1660, is probably the oldest Dutch building in South-East Asia. Its sturdy red-brick walls, massive wooden doors and window gratings have withstood the ravages of time.

The building is now occupied by Government offices. In an adjoining 300-year-old Dutch house is the Malacca Museum, with a variety of artefacts – few in number, but interesting – illustrating the history of Malacca.

Location
Jalan Laksamana

Tranquera Mosque

This 150-year-old mosque on the coast road to the north of Malacca is an unusual example of Islamic architecture in Malaysia. While most mosques follow Arab models, this one – a building of several storeys with a saddle-shaped pagoda roof – is modelled on the architecture of Sumatra (Indonesia).

This style, developed by the Minangkabau ethnic group on Sumatra, was brought to Malacca by Sumatrans who conquered south-western Malaysia during the Malay migration towards the end of the first millennium A.D.

Location
Jalan Tranquera

Open to visitors
Outside times of prayer

The interior of the mosque is very simple; the walls are faced with fine decorative tiles. There is a mausoleum said to contain the remains of Sultan Temenggong, who ceded Singapore to Stamford Raffles in 1819.

*Mandai Orchid Gardens

Location
Mandai Lake Road

Buses
171

Opening times
Daily 9 a.m–6 p.m.

The Mandai Orchid Gardens are the largest of their kind in Singapore, with an area of 4 hectares (10 acres), and have the widest range of species. The finest orchids of South-East Asia are cultivated here and exported all over the world. The gardens are situated on a hillside surrounded by primeval forest.
The total export of orchids from Singapore amounts to more than 3 million a year.

*Markets

Singapore would not be a true Asian city without its markets. The idyllic street markets and street kitchens, however, have had to give way to modernisation and have been poured into sterile concrete.

Chinatown

The happy chance, by which markets once spread over every empty spot in Chinatown, has been restrained by the new Kreta Ayer Complex in Sago Lane, in the very place where the death houses used to provide their service for the poor. The early morning market is open daily from six to ten and the night market, the Pasar Malam, from six to ten. The hygienic setting, however, has not altered the exotic variety of merchandise. Here are sold various Chinese medicines, even the sight of which may sometimes be too much for a Western stomach (perhaps a decoction of seahorses in wine, seasoned with powdered rhinoceros horn as an aphrodisiac?). The snakes which can be seen squirming about in a cage are also destined for the cooking-pot. The grasshoppers beside them serve both as delicacies for human consumption and for the nourishment of caged songbirds.

Fish markets

There are many fish markets in Singapore, but the most picturesque is the one at Jurong (see entry), which has a daily turnover of some 200 tonnes. On account of the high turnover the market is strictly controlled. Visitors unconnected with the trade need an official permit and tourists are, therefore, recommended to visit the fish market at Ponggol, which is open every day from 3 a.m., near the Hougang housing complex. Sharks, the fins of which are used to make the delicately flavoured shark's-fin soup, are now a rarity. Lobsters and giant prawns, however, are common throughout South-East Asia

Serangoon Market

This traditional market is now held in the Zhu Jiao Complex in Serangoon Road. There are sections for the Muslims, whose meat must be ritually slaughtered; here, too, there is a trading outpost of India, and of course all the colour and variety of Chinese food which, from what we hear, includes everything from the water, the land and the air, except submarines, tanks

The Mandai Orchid Gardens . . .

. . . with the largest collection of orchids in Singapore

and aeroplanes, since no one has yet devised a suitable marinade for them! The market is open in the morning and evening.

Cuppage Road Market

This market, which handles merchandise from all over the world, has also been transferred to a permanent building. Perishable goods which will not keep fresh are sold in tins – great mountains of tins. Here, too, there are Chinese hot-food stalls.

Handicraft Centre

The Singapore Tourist Promotion Board organises on Mondays, Tuesdays, Wednesdays and Sundays from 6 to 10 p.m. an open street market in the Handicraft Centre at Tudor Court. On Sundays between 11 a.m. and 6 p.m. there is also a flower market here.

Memorial Hall/Victoria Theatre   D4

Location
High Street

Buses
CBD 1

This colonial-style building was erected in 1854 as the Town Hall of the young town of Singapore, and in 1860 was converted to another use as the colony's first permanent theatre. The Memorial Hall (officially the Victoria Memorial Hall) is used as a ballroom as well as a theatre for both popular and classical productions.

Opposite the Memorial Hall is the Supreme Court.

Merlion Park   D4

Location
On Singapore River

Buses
142, 173, 174

At the outflow of the Singapore River into the Singapore Strait, in a small park, stands an 8 m (26 ft) high figure of a merlion, the lion-like sea monster said to have appeared 700 years ago to Prince Sang Nila Utama, who gave Singapore its name. The merlion is now the emblem of the island republic (see facing photograph).

From the park there are charming views of the harbour and its hundreds of junks.

---

*Mount Faber   F1

Rising to a mere 120 m (395 ft) above sea-level, Mount Faber can hardly be called a mountain; but it is high enough to afford fine views of the city of Singapore, some of the offshore islands and, in clear weather, of the Indonesian island of Sumatra. At night the city below the hill is transformed into a bluish unreality, a sea of lights, occasionally traversed by the flashing navigation lights of jumbo jets approaching the airport. Those who find the evening air too cool for them can watch the spectacle from the comfort of a restaurant.

On Mount Faber is the mainland station of the cableway to Sentosa Island (see entry).

The merlion, emblem of Singapore, in Merlion Park ▶

Viewing platform, Mount Faber

View of Singapore from Mount Faber

National Museum C4

The National Museum of Singapore is in three sections, all of which are of great interest – the Museum proper, the Art Gallery and the Haw Par Jade Collection.

The Museum has interesting collection of the fauna and flora of Singapore, archaeological material and Malay arts and crafts. The Art Gallery displays pictures and decorative art by local artists.

The Jade Collection was assembled and bequeathed to the state by the brothers Aw Boon Haw (the "Tiger") and Aw Boon Par (the "Leopard"), who made a fortune from their Tiger Balm medicine (see under Notable Personalities and the entries for Tiger Balm Garden and House of Jade).

The treasures on display include 384 pieces of jade, valuable Chinese porcelain and Italian marble statues. The collection is one of the finest of its kind in the whole of South-East Asia.

Location
Stamford Road

Buses
7, 13, 14, 16, 124, 140, 168, 171, 173, 174, CBD 1

Opening times
Daily 10.30 a.m.–7 p.m.

National Stadium B6

The National Stadium of Singapore, on Jalan Besar, covers an area of 60 hectares (150 acres) and can accommodate 50,000 visitors. It cost 50 million Singapore dollars to construct. In addition to the usual facilities for both indoor and outdoor sports there are judo rooms, squash courts and tennis and badminton courts. All the facilities provided are in line with Olympic standards. Associated with the Stadium is a sports medicine research centre.

Included within the complex are restaurants, exhibition rooms and a small theatre.

Location
Jalan Besar

Buses
14, 16

National University A1

The University of Singapore was founded in 1905 as King Edward VII College; now known as the National University of Singapore, it has faculties covering arts, science and technology and ranks with the best universities in the world.

The main part of the University (145 hectares (360 acres)) is at Kent Ridge, in the western part of the island. It has a fine art collection and a large library.

The colonial-style buildings date back to 1823, when Stamford Raffles established Singapore's first educational institution.

Location
Kent Ridge/Bukit Timah Hill

Buses
124, 173, 174; change to 33 at North Bridge Road

Night Markets

The traditional night markets, which used to change their location very frequently, have been integrated into the modern covered markets.

Chinatown: Kreta Ayer Complex, Sago Lane, daily 6–10 p.m.
Serangoon Market: Zhu Jiao Complex, Serangoon Road, daily 6–10 p.m.
Cuffage Road Market, daily 6–10 p.m.
Handicraft Centre, Tudor Court, Sundays, Mondays, Tuesdays and Wednesdays 6–10 p.m.

Opening times
Daily 6–10 p.m.

National University of Singapore

Padang

Location
St Andrew's Road

Buses
CBD 1

Padang is the Malay word for plain or open space, and is applied in any South-East Asian town to an area or space which has played a central part in its history and is still the centre of the town's life.

When Stamford Raffles first stepped ashore here in 1819 he had to make his way through a dense mangrove swamp, undeterred by the human skulls which littered the ground – macabre relics of the activities of the pirates of the South China Sea. The first area of open ground which could be traversed without the help of a bush knife was the open space now known as the Padang, which became the cradle of modern Singapore. Once the parade ground of British troops, it has long been the great meeting-place of Singapore society, still popularly known as "Scandal Point", the place for exchanging local news and gossip.

The annual parades held here on the Queen's Birthday came to an abrupt end in 1942 with the Japanese occupation of Singapore, and even after the Japanese surrender in 1945 things were never quite the same again. The Padang is now the scene of parades by Singapore's military forces, youth organisations and sports associations on the republic's National Day (9th August).

Round the Padang are monuments recalling the days of colonial rule – the Raffles statue in Empress Place, the

A stall in one of Singapore's night markets ▶

Shadow-play in Pasir Panjang Paradise

Victoria Memorial Hall and Theatre, Parliament House, City Hall, the Supreme Court and St Andrew's Cathedral (see those entries).

*Pasir Panjang Paradisa

Location
Pasir Panjang Road

Buses
143

Opening times
Daily at 11.30 a.m.

Admission charge

Every day at 11.30 a.m. the Pasir Panjang Paradisa is the scene of a performance in which the cultural life and traditions of Singapore's multi-racial society are presented in concentrated form.

The programme includes Chinese, Indian and Malay dances, bersilat (the Malay art of self-defence), classical Chinese music and Indian snake-charming.

Seats can be booked through the offices of the Singapore Tourist Promotion Board (see under Practical Information).

People's Park Centre   D3

Location
Chinatown/Eu Tong Sen Street

Buses
124, 143, 173, 174

The People's Park Centre contains under one roof a kind of mini-Singapore. In this five-storey complex, built on the site of an old market area destroyed by fire in 1960, are to be found doctors and beauty salons, hot-food stalls and hundreds of shops offering every conceivable variety of wares, from antiques to zoo animals. The Centre is open from 11 a.m. to 10 p.m.

People's Park Centre – a mini-Singapore under one roof

Racecourse

See Turf Club

Raffles Hotel   C4

The Raffles Hotel is one of the last nostalgic symbols of the British colonial era. When Sir Stamford Raffles gave his name to the hotel it was still surrounded by the jungle. The last tiger was seen here in 1902.
The Raffles, one of the most famous of British colonial hotels, has numbered among its visitors many distinguished people, including royalty. Among the celebrated writers who have stayed here are Somerset Maugham, Rudyard Kipling and Noel Coward. The architecture of the buildings, which are grouped around a central courtyard with palm trees, seems over elaborate, but the hotel with its old worn cane chairs and enormous rooms attracts very many tourists, who appreciate its traditional colonial atmosphere.

Location
Beach Road

Buses
7, 14, 16, CBD 1

Raffles Place   D4

Raffles Place has long been one of Singapore's more exclusive shopping areas. The fabrics, the jewellery, the optical and electronic goods and the watches sold in this area cater for the more discriminating tastes, which must be accompanied by a correspondingly well-filled wallet.

Buses
7, 14, 16, CBD 1

Raffles Hotel

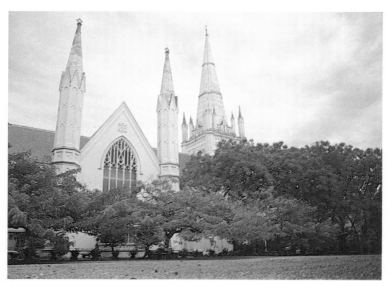

St Andrew's Cathedral

St Andrew's Cathedral   D4

St Andrew's Anglican Cathedral, built by Indian prisoners in 1843–46, is a neo-Gothic building with tall stained-glass windows and all the appearance of an English village church. It has a memorial window of 1861 commemorating Sir Stamford Raffles, "the illustrious founder of the settlement of Singapore".

When the Cathedral was built there was a popular belief, not yet forgotten, that the site was haunted by evil spirits who could be appeased only by an offering of 30 human heads.

Location
Coleman Street/St Andrew's Road

Buses
124, 173, 174

St John's Islands

After sailing through the Straits of Malacca on 6 February 1819 Stamford Raffles made his first landing in these islands, before crossing over to the main island of Singapore with a small advance party.

The islands, which are occupied by Malay fishermen, are very popular with bathers.

Boats return about 1 hour after departure from World Trade Centre.

Buses
143 to World Trade Centre

Boats
From World Trade Centre
Mon.–Sat. 10 a.m., 1.30 p.m.
Sun and holidays 9, 10,
11.20 a.m. 12.20, 1.40,
2.40, 4, 5, and 7.20 p.m.

Seletar Reservoir

Like the MacRitchie Reservoir (see entry), the Seletar Reservoir has been developed as a recreation area. It is Singapore's largest reservoir, with a capacity of almost 24,000 million litres (5300 million gallons).

There is an outlook tower which affords magnificent views of the surrounding area. The zoo, opened in 1973, can be seen on an electric tram which runs through the gardens.

Location
Mandai Lake Road

Buses
171

*Sentosa Island   G1

Formerly known as Pulau Blakang Mati, the island was occupied during the British colonial period by forts, but after the British withdrawal (1967) it was developed as a resort island under the more attractive name of Sentosa ("tranquillity"). It now attracts something like a million visitors every year. There is a 150-room luxury hotel with conference facilities for 1000 people. The island can be reached by cableway from Mount Faber, and there is a ferry service between Jardine Steps and the Sentosa Ferry Terminal.

A monorail runs round the main features of interest on the island, offering superb views of the scenery and introducing visitors to the topography and vegetation of the tropical world – swamps, mangrove forests, crocodile pools and the biotopes of the coastal regions.

The island's sports and recreation facilities include a roller-skating rink and two 18-hole championship golf-courses.

Bus
143 to World Trade Centre

Ferry
From World Trade Centre;
daily 7.30 a.m.–10 p.m.
every 15 minutes.

Cableway
From Mount Faber;
Mon.–Sat. 10 a.m.–7 p.m.
Sun. and pub. holidays
9 a.m.–7 p.m.

Sports and recreation facilities

63

Swimming Lagoon, Sentosa Island

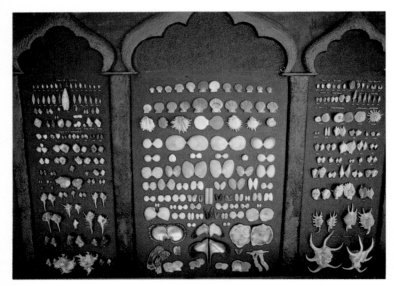

In the Coralarium, Sentosa Island

Carmelite Monastery CENTRAL BUSINESS DISTRICT

Telok Blangah Newtown

Spottiswoode Park

Mount Faber Scenic Park

St. Theresa

Singapore

Railway Station

Keramat

Empire Dock

Keppel Club

Market

Cable Car Station

Signal Station

Shipping Office

Pulau Hantu

P.S.A. Towers

World Trade Centre

P.S.A. Gate 1

Keppel

Harbour

Pulau Selegu

Fort Siloso

Mount Siloso

Pulau Brani

Musical Fountain

Pier

Selat

Sengkir

Berghala Reping

Carlton Hill

Cable Car Station

Art Centre

Maritime Museum

Mount Serapong

Sentosa

Camping

Swimming

Island

Golf-course

Lagoon

Marina

Golf-course

Coralarium

Sungei Blakang Mati

Sentosa Beach

Sentosa Island

500 m
550 yds

The Lagoon is 1·2 km (¾ mile) long and 137 m (450 ft) deep. At the east end of the lagoon is a boating marina and at the west end a camping site.

Swimming Lagoon

There is a Musical Fountain whose numerous sprays are synchronised with changing patterns of colour and a varied musical accompaniment.

Musical Fountain

The Maritime Museum illustrates the development of the port of Singapore and has displays of fishing techniques.

Maritime Museum

The Coralarium (area 1·2 hectares (3 acres)) displays a representative cross-section of the marine life of the South China Sea. Well worth seeing is "The Souls of the Sea" (Dari Laut), one of the largest shell collections in the world.

Coralarium Shell Collection

The collection displayed in the Art Centre includes contemporary oil-painting, Chinese sculpture, batik-work and pottery from South-East Asia.

Art Centre

The Surrender Chamber in the Wax Museum re-creates the

Surrender Chamber

signing of the Japanese surrender document at the end of the Second World War.

Fort Siloso

Fort Siloso, built in 1880, is one of the last of Singapore's coastal fortifications still preserved. During the Second World War the Japanese used it as a prisoner of war camp.
It contains an interesting Gun Museum.

Singapore River

D1–4

Buses
CBD 1, 124, 173, 174

The 3 km (2 mile) long Singapore River flows into the South China Sea. Thanks to its strategic situation the river, which was the island's first harbour and now leads into Keppel Harbour (see entry), is the scene of constant activity as a market and trading centre on the water. Here Stamford Raffles, looking for a suitable place to establish a trading settlement, first landed on the island of Singapore.

The hundreds and hundreds of sampans, as the bumboats and junks navigated by *swalos* (labourers) are called, which used to tranship goods to the warehouses by the Singapore River, have now been confined to a special section of Keppel Harbour.

**Siong Lim See Monastery

Location
Toa Payoh Housing Estate

Buses
64, 65, 92, 106, 111; change to 146 at Dhoby Ghout

This Twin Grove of the Lotus Mountain Temple is one of the most magnificent Buddhist temples in South-East Asia. Built between 1904 and 1910 in traditional Chinese style, it is said to be modelled in some respects on the Imperial Palace in Peking.

At the entrance to the temple are gigantic figures of the Four Kings of Heaven, each treading a demon under foot. They are the divine guardians of the sanctuary, protecting it against all evil that may approach from any of the cardinal points.

Beyond these is the Laughing Buddha, a great favourite with the Singapore Chinese, who do not regard their religion as a matter of deadly seriousness. Beside him is the mighty Wei T'o, defender of the faith.

In the innermost chamber, the holy of holies, is a figure of the Buddha deep in meditation. In the rear hall Kuan Yin, goddess of mercy, watches over the oldest part of the temple, which overlooks tranquil gardens. This small wooden shrine has fine wall-paintings. The side altars and recesses have a profusion of works of religious art, notable among them the marble Buddha figures from Thailand.

The temple is rich in good omens and in legends related to them. It is said, for example, that some years ago a poor trishaw-man fell asleep in front of the stone lion at the entrance and dreamed that the lion came to life and told him that he would win a great prize in a lottery: whereupon he bought a ticket, won 140,000 Singapore dollars and was able to return to China a rich man.

Entrance to Siong Lim See Monastery ▶

**Sri Mariamman Temple   E3

Location
South Bridge Road

Buses
124, 143, 173, 174

The Hindu Temple of Sri Mariamman was built between 1827 and 1843 by an Indian merchant who came to Singapore in a cargo vessel, the "Indiana". The labour force for its construction was provided by Indian convicts.

The imposing façade with its host of small sculptured figures depicts the deeds of the goddess Kali and scenes from Hindu mythology. Every evening at six o'clock the mystical music which accompanies the service is diffused over the surrounding area.

The interior of the temple, under its richly decorated domes, is a riot of ornament and gilding glorifying a host of Hindu divinities. In association with the Hindu Festival of Thimithi (see Practical Information – Festivals) the Fire Walking Ceremony takes place here in October or November according to the lunar calendar.

*Sultan Mosque   C5

Location
North Bridge Road/Arab Street

Bus
13

Open to visitors
Outside times of prayer

The Sultan Mosque was built by the last Sultan of Singapore, Iskandar Shah. Stamford Raffles donated 3000 dollars out of his own pocket towards its construction.

This is the religious centre of Singapore's Muslim population. It has 14 gates, at which red carpets are laid for the Friday prayers.

The interior is decorated with calligraphic Arabic inscriptions. It is paved with green and gold marble.

Sultan's Tomb

See Fort Canning Hill

Supreme Court   D4

Location
St Andrew's Road

Buses
CBD 1

In a proclamation of 1823 Stamford Raffles declared all men equal in the eyes of the law; and four years later, in 1827, Singapore's first court of law was established in a small bungalow. The present Supreme Court building was brought into use in 1937. It occupies the site of the old Europe Hotel, the meeting-place until 1932 of the Singapore upper crust. In Graeco-Roman style, it has a façade lined with slender Corinthian columns and is crowned by a tall and imposing dome.

The building now also houses the municipal administration (City Hall).

*Tanglin Road   B1

The Tanglin Road area is one of the more select districts of Singapore. Its long line of Tudor-style half-timbered buildings

The lavishly sculptured façade of the Sri Mariamman Temple ▶

Tanglin Road

Sultan Mosque: exterior . . .

. . . and the faithful at prayer

Supreme Court

Tanglin Road

is now occupied by expensive shops. Close by are the Botanic Gardens (see entry).

Here, too, is the head office of the Singapore Tourist Promotion Board (see under Practical Information).

Buses
7, 13, 14, 23, 64, 106, 111, 132, 132A, 174, 390, CBD 1

** Temple of a Thousand Lights
(officially the Sakya Muni Buddha Gaya Temple)

A4

When the young Buddhist monk Vutthisasara came to Singapore from his native Siam (Thailand) he resolved to build a temple to honour the Buddha, the Enlightened One. In the mid 1970s he died at the age of 94, his life's work accomplished: the Temple of a Thousand Lights was completed, and he had spread his doctrines of the Buddha in Singapore by his teaching and his preaching.

The temple is built on the model of a Siamese *wat* (monastery). Its central figure is a huge figure of the Buddha, standing some 15 m (50 ft) high and weighing some 300 tons, which is surrounded after dark by a nimbus of lights, said to number a thousand.

Round the base of the figure are scenes from the life of the Buddha, and the temple contains a precious relic, a piece of bark from the bodhi tree under which the Buddha attained Enlightenment. There is also a mother-of-pearl replica of the Buddha's footprint, copied from the one on Adam's Peak in Sri Lanka (Ceylon).

The entire temple, down to the tigers guarding the gate, was built by Vutthisasara with his own hands.

Location
Race Course Road

Buses
23, 64, 65, 106, 111, 198

Opening Times
9 a.m.–4.30 p.m.

71

Interior of the Temple of a Thousand Lights

Thian Hok Keng Temple

Thian Hok Keng Temple   E3

Thian Hok Keng, the Temple of Heavenly Happiness, is Singapore's oldest Chinese temple, built in 1840 as a resting-place and hostel for Chinese immigrants from Hokkien province.

The temple is dedicated to Ma-chu-po, Mother of Heavenly Sages in Chinese mythology. In earlier days every Chinese junk carried a small shrine in honour of the goddess. The temple is still a resting-place for Chinese seamen, dockworkers and old coolies. It has rich carved ornament and fine lacquer-painting.

Location
Telok Ayer Street

Bus
CBD 1 to Shenton Way

*Tiger Balm Gardens (Haw Par Villa)

This Confucian Madame Tussaud's or Disneyland is an immense and colourful advertising display devoted to glorifying the product after which the gardens are named, on a lavish and uninhibited scale such as could only be found in Asia.

The many acres of the gardens are filled with gaudy representations, in plaster, concrete and papier mâché, of scenes from Chinese mythology, outsize jungle animals, a plump and jolly Buddha, American, Greek and Italian themes, scenes from Chinese country life and the life of Singapore's streets, often with a moralising or didactic slant. One theme which is constantly hammered in, however, is the virtues of Tiger Balm – a specific against gout, toothache and other

Location
Pasir Panjang Road

Bus
143

Distance
9 km (6 miles) from city centre

Opening times
Daily 8 a.m.–6 p.m.

In the Tiger Balm Gardens, the "Confucian Madame Tussaud's"

ailments – and other products of the same firm, recommended for every conceivable purpose.

The Tiger Balm Gardens were established after the Second World War by the brothers Aw Boon Haw and Aw Boon Par (see Notable Personalities), who had made millions from the sale of Tiger Balm – still a very popular household remedy which proves effective against a variety of aches and pains.

The Aw brothers also devoted part of their fortune to various good causes, including the provision of free coffins for the poor, and presented their valuable collection of jade to the state (see House of Jade).

There are various restaurants and stalls selling drinks in the gardens.

Turf Club (Racecourse)

Location
Bukit Timah Road

Buses
171, 173, 174

Times of race-meetings
See newspapers

Horses came to Singapore with the British, and the new sport of horse-racing made its début about 130 years ago. Not surprisingly, perhaps, for the Chinese passion for gambling and for competing comes second only to their interest in eating.

Wealthy Chinese businessmen, Malay princes and the British colony became members of the Turf Club of Singapore, on whose racecourse the much-sought-after Singapore Cup is still contested every year.

The stud farms of Singapore and Malaysia are world-famed, being particularly noted for breeding horses which can stand up to the tropical climate. During the race-meetings millions of dollars are staked, part of the money going into the legal lottery and thus into the state coffers, but some of it also going to line the pockets of the illicit bookmakers who batten onto the sport. Everyone bets, from well-to-do businessmen to respectable Chinese amahs (nurses or maids).

This is still a happy hunting ground of the Chinese secret societies (*thongs*), of which there are officially reported to be 37, divided into something like a hundred gangs. In 1959 it was estimated that some 60 per cent of all Singaporeans were connected with one or other of these societies, which are nowadays mainly involved in illegal betting and lotteries but which also dominate the lush night life of Singapore.

*Van Kleef Aquarium   C/D3

Location
Central Park

Buses
123, 143

Opening times
Daily; 9.30 a.m.–9 p.m.

Admission charge

This small aquarium contains some 4600 sea creatures of all kinds, including rare specimens from many parts of the world. Among them are the local "flame fish", sea-anemones, coral fish, polyps, king crabs, turtles and sea-snakes. Also of great interest are the various species of marine flora and corals.

The aquarium, originally based on the private collection of a former resident of Singapore, Mr K. van Kleef, was established in its present form in Central Park (George V Jubilee Park) in 1955.

Singapore is now one of the world's largest exporters of aquarium fishes and other sea creatures. A large firm dealing in aquarium specimens has its headquarters in the Cathay Building, and there are other aquarium shops in the surrounding area.

Practical Information

Airlines

Some 30 international airlines fly regular services to and from Singapore. There are direct flights from many European and American cities.

The national airline, Singapore Airlines, flies to 34 cities throughout the world, with direct flights to Auckland, London Heathrow, Los Angeles, Melbourne, Perth, San Fransisco and Sydney among other cities.

A list of all airlines with offices in Singapore can be found in the "yellow pages" of the telephone directory.

Air France
UTA, Ming Court Hotel, Tanglin Road, tel. 737 6355

Alitalia
268 Orchard Road, 18-00, Yen San Building, tel. 737 6966/ 737 3166

British Airways
Far East Plaza, Scotts Road, tel. 253 8444

Lufthansa
Tanglin Shopping Centre, Tanglin Road, tel. 737 4444 and 737 9222

PanAm
126 Raffles Quay, 01-03, Hong Leong Building, tel. 220 0711

Sabena
01-31, International Plaza, Anson Road, tel. 221 7010-1

Singapore Airlines
Airline House, 77 Robinson Road, 01-06, tel. 223 8888 or 545 6666

Swissair
03-18, Lucky Plaza, Orchard Road, tel. 737 7004 or 737 8133

See also Air travel

Airport

Singapore's new international airport on the Changi Peninsula was opened for traffic in July 1981, replacing the old Paya Lebar Airport, which was no longer able to handle the growing volume of traffic. Singapore Changi Airport is designed to meet Singapore's requirements into the 21st century, with a passenger and freight-handling capacity several times greater than that of the older airport.

Singapore Changi Airport

Within the airport terminal are restaurants, banks and exchange

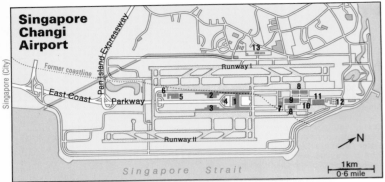

Singapore Changi Airport

Singapore (City)

Former coastline

Pan Island Expressway

East Coast Parkway

Police

Runway I

Runway II

Singapore Strait

N

1 km
0·6 mile

PASSENGER TERMINAL
1 Area 1
2 Area 2
3 Area 3

4 Control tower
5 Catering centre
6 Police
7 Transit post office

8 Freight terminals
9 Carriers
10 Bond warehouse
11 Hangar

12 Fuel Stores
13 Main fire station

offices, hotel reservation counters, car hire facilities, a post office, international telephones, duty-free shops, a tourist information office and baggage storage service. Duty-free goods may be purchased by both incoming and outbound passengers.

Air travel

There are numerous travel agencies in Singapore (see Travel agencies), including branches of the large international organisations, which offer a wide range of international tourist flights from Singapore. In this very competitive market visitors will do well to shop around and compare prices. Singapore Airlines and the Malaysian Airline System offer reasonably priced package trips to various destinations in South-East Asia. The national airlines of Singapore (SIA), Malaysia (MAS), Thailand (Thai International), Indonesia (Garuda) and the Philippines (Philippine Airlines) combine to offer some restricted fare round-trip flights to these ASEAN countries at reduced rates.

Animals

An import permit is required to bring either live or stuffed animals into Singapore. If a permit is granted there are strict quarantine requirements.
An export permit is required to take out cats, dogs and other live animals.
For information apply to diplomatic missions (see entry), tourist information offices (see Information) or the immigration authorities (see Travel documents).

Singapore's new international airport on the Changi Peninsula

Antiques

Singapore is one of the largest markets for antiques in the Far East, with a range extending from the artefacts of the many native peoples of South-East Asia through old Chinese furniture to expensive Chinese porcelain, sculpture and antique jewellery.

Although the export of antiques is subject to strict controls and restrictions in most countries in the region, items produced in Singapore can be exported without any problems.
Visitors taking Asian antiques from Singapore to another Asian country should take care to obtain a certificate of import in order to avoid possible difficulties when leaving the country.

Export

There are antique shops in all the large international hotels (though prices there are high), in most shopping centres (see Shopping centres), in department stores and in Orchard Road. Competition in this field is fierce, and it is well worth while comparing prices and bargaining vigorously.
A selection of shops:

Antique shops

Katong Antiqua,
208 East Coast Road
Specialises in Nonya antiques and Malacca and Chu porcelain

Paul Art Gallery,
G 14-A Supreme House
Carved jade, ivory, bronzes, lacquerware

77

Kwok Gallery,
Far East Shopping Centre,
Chinese antiques

C. K. Tang (House of Tang),
Orchard Road, Tanglin Shopping Centre,
Chinese antiques

Further antique shops can be found in the telephone directory
(yellow pages) under the heading "Antique dealers".

Warning

Unless you are an expert, do not buy expensive antiques
without advice from someone who knows about them.

Arrival in Singapore

By air

Most visitors now arrive by air (see Getting to Singapore) at
Singapore Changi Airport (see Airport).

Hotel reservations

Visitors who already have hotel reservations should confirm
them at the hotel reservation counter in the terminal building.
If they have no reservations they should make a booking at the
counter.

Transit passengers

Transit passengers who want to pay a quick visit to the city can
leave their heavy luggage in the left luggage office, which is
open 24 hours a day.

Porters

Porters can be hired at the airport. S$0·5 per article.

Transport to the city

There are hotel bus services between the airport and the various
international hotels. Tickets obtainable in the arrival hall. Bus
390.

Drugs

The possession or sale of dangerous drugs is subject to the
death penalty.

Warnings

Male visitors with long hair or hippie appearance may be
refused entry.
Smoking is prohibited in many public offices, taxis, buses, lifts,
cinemas, theatres and institutions. Infringement: 500 Singapore dollars. The dropping of litter – even a cigarette end –
can also bring a fine of up to 500 Singapore dollars.
It is forbidden to cross streets except at pedestrian crossings.

Arrival by rail

Singapore Station links the city with the Malaysian railway
system (KTM). Luggage can be deposited in the left luggage
office at the station.

Banks

Altogether 89 national and international banks operate in
Singapore, with a total of 288 branches, which can carry out all
kinds of banking transactions.
Singapore's central bank is the Monetary Authority of
Singapore, which fixes exchange rates daily.

Algemeene Bank Nederland NV, 2 Cecil Street

Asia Commercial Banking Corporation, 2 Mistri Road

Bangkok Bank, Bangkok Bank Building, 180 Cecil Street

Bank of America, Clifford Centre, 24 Raffles Place

Bank of China, Battery Road

Bank of Singapore, 101 Cecil Street

Chase Manhattan Bank, Shing Kwan House, 4 Shenton Way

Citibank, UIC Building, Shenton Way

Development Bank of Singapore, DBS Building, Shenton Way

First National Bank of Chicago, Wing On Life Building, 150 Cecil Street

Hongkong and Shanghai Banking Corporation, Ocean Building, 10 Collyer Quay

International Bank of Singapore, IBS Building, 31 Raffles Place

There are branches of Banks (open 24 hours a day) in the arrival hall, the departure hall and the main airport building.	At airport
There is a branch of the Overseas Union Bank (open Mon.–Fri. 9.30 a.m.–4 p.m., Sat. 9.30 a.m.–midday) in the office of the Singapore Tourist Promotion Board (see Information).	At Tourist Promotion Board
Banks are normally open from 10 a.m. to 3 p.m. Monday to Friday, 9.30 to 11.30 a.m. on Saturday.	Banking hours
Money can be changed at licensed exchange offices as well as in banks. They display the sign "Licensed money changer" and are to be found in most shopping centres. Their exchange rates are better than those offered in hotels, which charge a commission.	Exchange offices

Boat trips

Evening cruises in a Chinese junk Daily Duration: about 3 hours Booking: at Eastwind Organisation, Clifford Pier, tel. 533 3432; Watertours, Clifford Pier, tel. 914 519; or at any travel agent. Dinner on board is included.	Evening cruises
Daily at 10.30 a.m., 3 and 4 p.m. Departure: Clifford Pier Duration: about 2 hours	Harbour cruises
Cruises to Kusu and St John's Islands (see entries) are no	Island cruises

longer organised. However, they can be undertaken by ferry from the World Trade Centre on an individual basis.

See Sightseeing tours

City tours

Bus trips

Travel agencies in Singapore offer a wide range of coach trips into Malaysia.

To Malaysia

There are the following daily services by express bus:

Singapore–Johore
Several departures daily from Rochor Centre, Bencoolan Street

Singapore–Kuala Lumpur Express
9 a.m. and 9 p.m. (journey time 9 hours)
From New Bridge Road car park; Mara Company, tel: 221 6601

Singapore–Mersing (see Kota Tinggi)
9 and 10 a.m. (journey time 4 hours)
From New Bridge Road car park; Mara Company, tel: 221 6601

Singapore–Malacca Express
8, 9.30, and 11 a.m., 1, 2 and 3 p.m.
From New Bridge Road car park; Malacca–Singapore Express Co., tel: 223 8868

Camping

There are no camping sites in Singapore. Motor caravans are not admitted except in transit for loading on to a ship.

Car hire

Car hire firms are listed in the yellow pages of the telephone directory. In addition to the well-known international firms there are many local hire firms.
Rates for self-drive cars vary considerably from firm to firm, but in general range between 55 and 320 dollars per day and between 390 and 1920 dollars per week, with a mileage charge ranging between 40 cents and 1·20 dollars per kilometre. For periods longer than a week there are special rates.
Cars can also be hired for tours in Malaysia, with the facility of leaving the car in the larger Malaysian towns.

Foreign drivers of hire cars must produce both their national driving licence and an international driving licence.

Documents

Chemists

There are chemists' shops in almost all Singapore's shopping

◀ *A Chinese junk on the Singapore River*

centres. Chemists are listed under the heading "Pharmacies" in the yellow pages of the telephone directory.

Medicines without prescription

Most medicines are obtainable without a doctor's prescription. Visitors on special drugs should bring a supply with them. The proprietary names of drugs may differ from those used in the West.

Emergencies

In case of emergency dial 995.

Opening times

Chemists' shops are normally open from 9 a.m. to 6 p.m.

Church services

All churches and other places of worship are listed in the yellow pages of the telephone directory. For times of service ring the numbers given below.

Anglican

St Andrew's Cathedral, Coleman Street, tel. 337 6104

Baptist

Baptist Church, 90 Kings Road, tel. 466 4929

Inter-denominational

Salvation Army, 207 Clemenceau Avenue, tel. 737 9122

Lutheran

Queenstown Lutheran Church, 709 Commonwealth Drive, tel. 63 7866

Methodist

Wesley Church, 5 Fort Canning Road, tel. 336 1433

Presbyterian

Presbyterian Church, B & C Orchard Road, tel. 337 6681

Roman Catholic

Cathedral of the Good Shepherd, Queen Street, tel. 337 2036

Seventh Day Adventist

Seventh Day Adventist Church, 120 Balestier Road, tel. 256 4571

Jewish

Jewish Synagogue, Waterloo Street, tel. 336 0692
Reuben Manasseh Meyer Synagogue, Oxley Rise

Credit cards

Most shops in the shopping centres, department stores and shops catering for an international clientele accept the generally recognised credit cards (Euro Card, American Express, Asia Card, Visa, Carte Blanche, Dinner Club, Master Charge, etc.).

Currency

Currency regulations

The Singapore currency market is free and unrestricted, and deals in all currencies. Money can be changed at all banks, by licensed money-changers (see under Banks) and in hotels. Foreign currency can be brought in any form and unlimited amount.

The monetary unit is the Singapore dollar (S\$), which is divided into 100 cents.
There are bank notes for 1, 5, 10, 20, 50, 100, 500, 1000 and 10,000 dollars and coins in denominations of 1, 5, 10, 20 and 50 cents and 1 dollar.

Singapore's currency

Singapore's central bank, the Monetary Authority, has issued various specially minted silver and gold coins. Information from banks.

Special mintings

Rates in April 1985 (subject to fluctuation):
£1 sterling=S\$2·70   S\$1=37p
\$1 (US)=S\$2·23   S\$1=45c

Exchange rates

There is usually a better exchange rate for travellers' cheques than for cash.

Travellers' cheques

See entry

Credit cards

See Banks

Changing money

Customs regulations

Since Singapore is a free port, visitors can buy and export most goods free of duty.

Visitors over 18, except when coming from Malaysia, can bring in duty-free 1 litre of spirits, 1 litre of wine and 1 litre of beer, together with 200 cigarettes or 50 cigars or 250 grammes of tobacco. No duty is payable on personal effects.
Transit passengers who exceed these amounts must leave the excess at the customs.
Import authorisations are required for firearms, ammunition, animals whether live or stuffed, meat and meat products whether cooked or raw, live plants and seeds, poisons, vaccines, sera and controlled drugs.
Books and publications are subject to control.

Entry

Export authorisations are required for all items subject to import authorisation, as listed above.

Exit

See under Motoring

Motor vehicles

Information about the regulations applicable to seagoing vessels can be obtained from the Port of Singapore Authority (tel. 271 2211), Singapore Tourist Promotion Board offices abroad and diplomatic missions.

Arrival by private yacht

Department stores

Bobby-O Department Store,
Stamford Road
Open daily 10 a.m.–9 p.m.

C. K. Tang,
Orchard Road, Dynasty Hotel
Open Mon.–Sat. 9.30 a.m.–8.30 p.m.

Cortina,
Colombo Street, North Bridge Road
Open daily 10.30 a.m.–7 p.m.

Isetan,
Apollo Hotel, Havelock Road
Open daily 10 a.m.–9 p.m.

John Little,
ShoppingPlaza Singapura, Orchard Road
Open daily 10 a.m.–8 p.m.

John Little,
Plaza Singapura
Open Mon.–Sat. 10 a.m.–5.30 p.m., Sun. 10 a.m.–5 p.m.

Klasse,
Lucky Plaza, Orchard Road
Open daily 10 a.m.–10 p.m.

Metro Bukhit Timah,
Bukit Timah Plaza, Jalan Anak Bukit
Open daily 9.30 a.m.–10 p.m.

Metro Golden Mile,
Beach Road
Open daily 10 a.m.–9.30 p.m.

Metro Orchard,
Scotts Road
Open daily 9.30 a.m.–9.30 p.m.

Metro Supreme,
Supreme House, Penang Road
Open daily 10 a.m.–9.30 p.m.

O. G. Elite,
Plaza Singapura, Orchard Road
Open daily 11 a.m.–9.30 p.m.

Peter Chew's,
Penang Road, Supreme House
Open daily 10 a.m.–9 p.m.

Robinsons,
Orchard Road
Open Mon.–Wed. 9.45 a.m.–5.30 p.m.,
Thu. and Sat. 9.45 a.m.–8.30 p.m., Sun. 9.45 a.m.–5 p.m.

Scott's Plus,
Scotts Shopping Centre,
Scotts Road
Open daily 10 a.m.–9 p.m.

Yaohan Thomson,
Upper Thomson Road, Thomson Plaza
Open Mon.–Fri. 10 a.m.–8 p.m.,
Sat. and Sun. 9.30 a.m.–10 p.m.

Shopping centres   See entry

Diplomatic missions

High Commission, Tanglin Road, tel. 63 9333	United Kingdom
Embassy, 30 Hill Street, tel. 338 0251	United States
High Commission, 8th floor, Faber House, 230 Orchard Road, tel. 737 1322	Canada
High Commission, 25 Napier Road, tel. 737 9311	Australia
High Commission, 13 Nassim Road, tel. 235 9966	New Zealand

Since office hours vary, it is well to enquire by telephone when the particular office will be open. All diplomatic missions are closed on Saturdays. There is a 24-hour telephone service for emergencies.

Office hours

Doctors

For a list of all practising doctors, consult the yellow pages of the telephone directory under the heading "Medical practitioners". Dentists are listed under "Dental surgeons".
Many hotels have their own doctors, on call 24 hours a day.

Dress

Singapore, lying some 100 km (60 miles) north of the Equator, has average day temperatures of about 30 °C/86 °F and night temperatures that are not much lower. It is advisable, therefore, to take mainly light summer clothing. Man-made fibres, which are not particularly absorbent, should be avoided, particularly for close fitting underwear; the best material is cotton. Since most hotels and other buildings are air-conditioned, it is advisable to have a jacket or stole when spending some time, for example, in a restaurant.
Standards of dress in Singapore are very relaxed. In most restaurants – even the best ones – there is no requirement on men to wear a jacket and tie. For women, long-sleeved batik blouses in reasonably restrained patterns are perfectly acceptable.
If you have official business to transact, however, it is normal to wear a collar and tie.
Slovenly, hippie-like dress is not welcome in Singapore; nor are

T-shirts with suggestive inscriptions. Either of these is liable to bring the wearer into conflict with the authorities.
During the rainy season (December–March and June–September) an umbrella should form part of the visitor's equipment.

Electricity

200–240 volts AC, 50 cycles.

Emergency calls

General emergency call, fire, ambulance: dial 995
Police: dial 999

Ferry services

Ferry services to the islands off Singapore depart at irregular intervals from Clifford Pier, Jardine Steps and the World Trade Centre.

Northern islands

Departure from Ponggol Boatel (fast launches carrying 5 passengers). Information: tel 481 0031/2.
Facilities for water skiing.

Southern islands

Kusu Island, St John's Islands: see A to Z section

Pulau Hantu

Charter boats from Jardine Steps or Clifford Pier

Sentosa Island

See A to Z section

Festivals

With its multi-racial population, Singapore celebrates a great variety of colourful festivals. The dates of the festivals vary from year to year, since they are determined by different calendars – the lunar calendar for the Chinese, the Muslim calendar for the Malays and the Hindu calendar for the Indians.

Thaipusam

A Hindu festival. Penitents walk in procession, mortifying the flesh with skewers through their tongue and cheeks, from the Perumal Temple in Serangoon Road by way of Selegie Road, Dhoby Ghaut, Orchard Road and Clemenceau Avenue to the Chettiar Temple (see A to Z), returning in the evening by way of Maxwell Road, Robinson Road, Market Street, Cecil Street, Cross Street, New Bridge Street and River Valley Road. The procession is accompanied by well-wishers, chanting and dancing to the beat of drums.

Chinese New Year

During the month before the New Year Chinese families clean and redecorate their homes and hang up strips of red paper inscribed with luck-bringing formulae. The celebrations are seen at their best in Chinatown (see A to Z).

 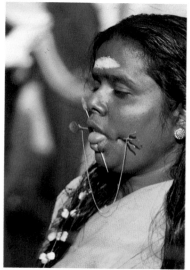

Mortification of the flesh at the Thaipusam Festival

A colourful procession through the city shortly after the Chinese New Year, with drums, decorated floats, Chinese music, stilt-walkers and lion and dragon dancers.

Chingay Parade

During these celebrations, held twice a year in many Chinese temples, spirit mediums pierce their tongue and cheeks with long needles, fall into a trance and give out special charms to worshippers. Chinese operas and puppet plays are performed in temple courtyards.
The celebrations are particularly impressive at the temples in Eng Hoon Street and Cumming Street.

Birthday of the Monkey God

Celebrated by a candlelight procession following a figure of Christ round St Joseph's Church in Victoria Street.

Good Friday

A spectacular competition, held when the north-east monsoon is blowing, with kites representing dragons, fish, butterflies, Malay "moon kites" and large Western kites participating.

International Kite Festival

Chinese families go to the cemeteries in Lornie Road, Upper Thomson Road and Lim Chu Kang Road to tidy up the graves of their ancestors and leave offerings of food and incense.

Ching Ming Festival

A Thai water festival during which images of Buddha are bathed in holy water.
Celebrated in the Ananda Metyarama Temple in Silat Road and the Sapthapuchaniyaram Temple in Holland Road.

Songkran Festival

A Taoist festival in which the Third Prince of the Lotus is honoured as a hero and wonder-worker. The child god,

Birthday of the Third Prince

Practical Information

carrying a magic bracelet in one hand and a spear in the other, rides on a "wheel of wind and fire". During the festival spirit mediums mortify the flesh. In the afternoon there is a procession through the streets.

Celebrated in the Taoist temple between Clarke Street and North Boat Quay.

Birthday of the Saint of the Poor

A figure of the Saint of the Poor (Kong Teck Choon Ong) is carried through the streets by Chinese workers, accompanied by spirit mediums with long needles through their cheeks and tongue.

The procession starts from the White Cloud Temple in Ganges Avenue, makes its way through the surrounding streets and returns to the temple.

Vesak Day

A Buddhist festival celebrating the birth, enlightenment and death of Buddha. Believers flock to the temples to pray, monks in their saffron robes recite prayers throughout the day, the poor are given food and birds are set free from their cages, in the assurance that Buddha will reward this good deed. At many temples there are candlelight processions and performances of traditional dramas.

The celebrations are particularly impressive in the Temple of a Thousand Lights (see A to Z).

Beginning of Ramadan

This is the start of the Muslim month of fasting, during which believers take no food or drink between sunrise and sunset. Special stalls set up in Bussorah Street, behind the Sultan Mosque, offer cakes and other delicacies to those who have just ended their fast.

Dragon Boat Festival

The Dragon Boat Festival commemorates an ancient Chinese poet, Qu Yuan, who drowned himself in protest against injustice and corruption. Special meat-filled rice dumplings wrapped in bamboo leaves are eaten during this festival, recalling the dumplings which fishermen were said to have thrown into the water to lure fish away from the poet's body. The rice dumplings (*chung*) can be bought in Chinatown during the festival.

Hari Raya Puasa

The end of Ramadan, marked by the first sighting of the new moon on the first day of the tenth month in the Muslim calendar. The faithful go to the mosque to pray, visit friends and relatives and celebrate the end of the fast with a substantial meal.

National Day

National Day (9 August), in honour of Singapore's achievement of independence, is celebrated with military parades, lion and dragon dances and various cultural events.

Market Festival

During the seventh month of the lunar calendar stall-holders in the city's markets lay out lavish displays of fruit and Chinese delicacies for the spirits of the dead. Chinese operas are performed in the streets, and spectators giving money to the performers are offered fruit in return.

Festival of the Hungry Ghosts

It is believed that during the seventh month the spirits of the dead return briefly to earth, and in order to propitiate them joss sticks are lit and offerings of food and "ghost money" are laid out. Chinese operas and puppet plays are performed in the streets.

Festival of the Hungry Ghosts

A Hindu festival which is celebrated in most temples. During the first three days the goddess Parvathi, consort of the god Shiva the Destroyer, is honoured. The next three days are devoted to Lakshmi, goddess of wealth and consort of Vishnu the Protector, and the last three days of the festival to Saraswathi, goddess of education and consort of Brahma the Creator.

The gods Shiva, Vishnu and Brahma make up the Hindu trinity. During the nine days of the festival there are performances of Indian music and dancing in the Chettiar Temple (7–10 p.m.). On the tenth day the end of the festival is marked by the Procession of the Silver Horse. Starting from the Chettiar Temple, it makes its way along River Valley Road, Kelliney Road, Orchard Road, Clemenceau Avenue and so back to the temple.

Navarathri Festival

This festival, celebrated in most mosques, is in honour of the pilgrimage to Mecca. It is a day of prayer, on which animals are ritually slaughtered and the meat distributed to the poor.

Those who have made the pilgrimage wear a white cap and are addressed as *haji* (if a man) or *hajiah* (if a woman).

Hari Raya Haji

According to a Chinese legend the conspirators who overthrew the tyrannous Mongol dynasty sent messages to one another hidden in moon cakes (round cakes containing lotus nuts, sweet red bean paste and sometimes salted egg yolk), and in commemoration of this the Chinese eat moon cakes on the night of the year on which the moon is believed to be at its fullest. The day is also celebrated with processions of gaily coloured paper lanterns.

Moon Cake Festival

Moon Cake Festival

Festival of the Nine Emperor Gods

During the ninth lunar month Taoist pilgrims, to the number of some 100,000, flock to the Tua Pek Kong Temple (see A to Z, Kusu Island), where they light joss sticks and candles and pray for prosperity, health and well-behaved children.
Both Chinese and Malays take part in the pilgrimage. Visitors who want to be present at this festival can take the ferry to accompany the procession of boats to Kusu Island.

Pilgrimage to Kusu Island

The Chinese honour the Nine Emperor Gods on the ninth day of the ninth lunar month, believing that they cure ailments and bring luck, wealth and long life. During the nine days of this festival many Chinese fast or mortify the flesh. Chinese operas are performed in the streets, and in the evening images of the gods are carried through the streets in splendidly decorated litters, accompanied by cymbals and drums and followed by crowds of worshippers bearing yellow flags.
The celebrations in the temple in Upper Serangoon Road (8 km (5 miles) away) and the Lorong Tai Seng are particularly impressive.

Festival of the Nine Emperor Gods

This Hindu fire-walking festival celebrates the greatness and purity of the goddess Durobadai. About three in the afternoon a procession leaves the Perumal Temple in Serangoon Road and makes its way by Selegie Road, Prinsep Street, Bras Basah Road and North Bridge Road to the Sri Mariamman Temple (see A to Z). About 4 p.m. devotees of the goddess walk across a pit of burning coals in fulfilment of their vows.

Thimithi

This Festival of Lights celebrates the victory of light over darkness, the triumph of good over evil. Oil-lamps are lit in all Hindu homes, and people dress in their best clothes and visit friends and relatives. The shrines in the temples are decorated and the altars laden with fruit, and an effigy of the god is carried in procession round the temple.

Deepavali

On the twelfth day in the third month of the Muslim calendar the Prophet's birthday is celebrated. Ceremonies are held in all mosques, and in the Koranic schools teachers tell of his life and achievements in Malay, Arabic, Tamil and English. Visitors are welcome. About seven in the evening passages from the "Berzanji", an account of Mohammed's life, are read in all mosques.
The most impressive celebrations are those in the Sultan Mosque (see A to Z).

Maulidin Nabi

Christmas is a public holiday in Singapore.

Christmas

Folk traditions

In spite of the rapid pace of Westernisation and modernisation which is so visible everywhere in Singapore the folk traditions of its various races are still very much alive: see under Festivals, above. Information about events of folk interest can be obtained from the Tourist Promotion board (see under Information, below).

In spite of Western influences folk traditions are still very much alive in Singapore

Regular folk entertainments are organised in the following establishments:

Instant Asia,
Paradise, Pasir Panjang Road
Daily at 11 a.m.

ASEAN Cultural Extravaganza,
Hin's Heavenly Cookhouse, Hilton Hotel
Daily at 7.30 p.m.

Malayan Night,
Swimming-pool terrace, Mandarin Hotel
Daily at 7 p.m.

Ming Cultural Night,
Ming Palace, Ming Court Hotel
Tuesday and Thursday at 7.30 p.m.

Raffles Malayan Night Revue,
Ballroom, Raffles Hotel
Daily at 8 p.m.

Villa Saujana Cultural Show,
Villa Saujana, Loyang
Daily at 7 p.m.

Chinese operas

There are regular performances of Chinese street operas. Information from Tourist Promotion Board (see under Information, below).

Food and drink

The cuisine of Singapore reflects the multi-racial nature of its society; but visitors who want to enjoy the fascination of Asian food must get away from the international hotels. Resounding names and luxurious settings are not always a guarantee of good food, and the gourmet must pursue a selective path among the city's hundreds of restaurants and hawker food stalls (street kitchens). Public health controls in Singapore are so strict that it is perfectly safe to eat food from even the smallest of these food stalls. Visitors from the West should, however, be cautious when sampling hot and highly spiced dishes for the first time.

Food

The jungles of South-East Asia yield a great range of delicious fruits which are almost unknown in the West.
Durian, the "king of fruits", is an evil-smelling fruit with a distinctive taste which has many devotees.
Rambutan is a succulent white-fleshed fruit similar in taste to a litchi.
Other fruits which will appeal to visitors are mangoes, bananas, starfruit, pomelos and mangosteens.
Buah susu is a milky-white drink made from passion fruit.

Local fruits

The ordinary water supply is drinkable, but highly chlorinated. Western alcoholic drinks are obtainable in all restaurants and hotel bars.

Drink

See entry

Restaurants

Getting to Singapore

Overland
Although Singapore is connected with Asia Highway A 1, which is planned to run from London to Vietnam, it cannot be reached by the overland route, since the highway is interrupted in Burma.

From Europe

By air
This is the usual means of approach. Most European airlines have direct flights to Singapore. The flight from London takes $14\frac{1}{2}$–16 hours.

By air: direct flight from a number of cities. See Airlines, above.

From North America

By rail
There are sleeper trains with air-conditioning nightly from the Malaysian capital Kuala Lumpur (connecting with trains from Bangkok) to Singapore.
There are also day trains. The journey takes about 9 hours.

From Malaysia

By car
There is an excellent motor road from Kuala Lumpur to Singapore via the Causeway from Johor Bahru. About 7 hours.

By bus
There are several express buses daily between Kuala Lumpur and Singapore. About 8 hours.

Practical Information

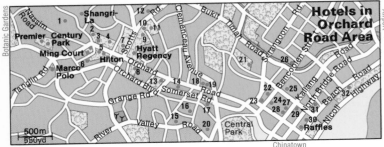

• HOTELS

1 Ladyhill	9 York	17 Cockpit	25 South East Asia
2 Mimosa	10 Goodwood Park	18 Grand Central	26 White House
3 Orchard	11 Queen's	19 Supreme	27 Ramada Tai-Pan
4 Negara	12 Asia	20 Oberoi Imperial	28 Victoria
5 Singapura	13 Mandarin	21 Savoy	29 New Empress
6 Boulevard	14 Phoenix	22 Bencoolen	30 Metropole
7 Holiday Inn	15 Mitre	23 Strand	31 New 7th Storey
8 Irama	16 Lloyd House	24 South Asia	32 Pan Pacific

By boat
There are passenger ships several times a week between Port
Klang in Malaysia and Singapore, continuing to Eastern
Malaysia (North Borneo).

Hospitals

Singapore General Hospital, Outram Road: tel. 222 3322.
Most of the large hotels have their own doctor on call (see
Doctors).

Hotels

Singapore's hotels, judged by international standards, rank
among the best in the world. It is advisable for visitors to book
before leaving home. All hotels make a service charge of 10 per
cent in addition to the Government tax of 3 per cent.

Hotel categories

In view of the increases in hotel tariffs due to inflation it is not
possible in the following list of hotels to give exact rates. The
hotels are listed in alphabetical order in three categories: luxury,
first-class and modest.

Luxury hotels

*Apollo (340 r.), Havelock Road, tel. 733 2081
*Apollo Sentosa (161 rooms), Sentosa Island, tel. 633 377
*Century Park (462 rooms), Nassim Hill, tel. 737 9677
*Cockpit (220 rooms), Oxley Rise, tel. 737 9111
*Crown Prince (303 rooms), 270 Orchard Road, Tel: 732 1111
*Goodwood Park (300 rooms), Scotts Road, tel. 737 7411
*Holiday Inn (600 rooms), Scotts Road, tel. 737 7966
*Holiday Inn Park View (320 rooms), Cuppage/Cavenagh
Roads, Tel 737 7966
*Hyatt Regency (824 rooms), Scotts Road, tel. 733 1188
*Mandarin (700 rooms), Orchard Road, tel. 737 4411

°Marco Polo (605 rooms), Tanglin Circus, tel. 474 7141
°Meridien Hotel (419 rooms), 100 Orchard Road, tel: 733 8855
°New Otani Hotel, (408 rooms), 177 River Valley Road, tel: 337 0658
°Pavilion Inter-Continental (450 rooms) I, Cuscaden Road, tel: 733 8888
°Shangri-La (700 rooms), Orange Grove Road, tel. 737 3644
°Singapore Hilton (410 r.), Orchard Road, tel. 737 2233
°York (408 rooms), Mount Elizabeth, tel. 737 0511

Asia (140 r.), Scotts Road, tel. 737 8388   First-class hotels
Boulevard (220 r.), Orchard Boulevard, tel. 737 2911
Duke (170 r.), Meyer Road, tel. 345 3311
Equatorial (224 r.), Bukit Timah Road, tel. 732 0431
Garden (96 r.), Balmoral Road, tel. 235 3344
Great Eastern (151 r.), MacPherson Road, tel. 284 8244
King's (175 r.), Havelock Road, tel. 733 0011
Ladyhill (180 r.), Ladyhill Road, tel. 737 2111
Ming Court (300 r.), Orchard Road, tel. 737 1133
Miramar (214 r.), Havelock Road, tel. 733 0222
Negara (104 r.), Claymore Drive, tel. 737 0811
Oberoi Imperial, (561 r.), Jalan Rumbia, tel. 737 1666
Orchid Inn (122 r.), Dunearn Road, tel. 250 3322
Pan Pacific (350 r.), Beach Road, tel. 297 2592
Peninsula (315 r.), Somerset Road, tel. 337 8091
Phoenix, (400 r.), Somerset Road, tel. 737 8666
Premier (30 r.), Nassim Hill, tel. 235 5111
Queen's (61 r.), Mount Elizabeth, tel. 737 6088
Raffles (127 r.), Beach Road, tel. 337 8041
Royal Ramada (321 r.), Newton Road, tel. 253 4411
Sea View (460 r.) Amber Close, tel. 345 2222
Tai-Pan (267 r.), Victoria Street, tel. 336 0811

Singapore has many hotels which offer a more modest standard   Modest hotels
of facilities but are very clean.

YMCA, 8 Canning Rise, tel. 337 7639   YMCA/YWCA
YWCA, 8 Fort Canning Road, tel. 336 0726

Information

Singapore Tourist Promotion Board,   In the United Kingdom
33 Heddon Street,
London W1R 7LB
Tel. (01) 437 0033

Singapore Tourist Promotion Board,   In the United States
Suite 1008, 10th floor,
342 Madison Avenue,
New York NY 10173
Tel. (212) 687 0358

Singapore Tourist Promotion Board,
251 Post Street, Suite 308,
San Fransisco CA 94108
Tel. (415) 391 8476

Singapore Tourist Promotion Board,   In Australia
8th floor, Goldfields House,
1 Alfred Street, Circular Quay,
Sydney NSW 2000
Tel. 241 3771

Practical Information

In New Zealand	Singapore Tourist Promotion Board,
	P.O. Box 279,
	87 Queen Street,
	Auckland 1
	Tel. (9) 793708

In Singapore

Singapore Tourist Promotion Board (STPB),
131 Tudor Court, Tanglin Road,
Singapore 1024
Tel. 235 6611
Open Mon.–Fri. 8 a.m.–5 p.m.; Sat. 8 a.m.–1 p.m.

The Singapore Tourist Promotion Board (STPB) is the Government tourism authority. It is responsible for planning tourism within Singapore and promoting its tourist industry abroad. The Board provides information and excellent tourist literature for visitors to Singapore (of whom there were just under 3 million in 1984).
The STPB also deals with complaints from visitors who have suffered cheating or discourteous treatment in Singapore.

Conference planning

For assistance in the planning and running of conferences in Singapore apply to:
Singapore Convention Bureau,
135 Tudor Court, Tanglin Road
Tel. 235 6611

Trade fairs and exhibitions

For information on trade fairs and exhibitions apply to:
Singapore Tourist Promotion Board, tel. 235 6611
World Trade Centre, tel. 271 2211

Inoculations

See Travel Documents

Languages

The language of business and administration is English. The mother tongues of Singapore's different races – Mandarin and Chinese dialects, Tamil and Malay – are used for teaching (until 1987) up to the secondary school stage, but even then only as second languages.
The post-war generation speaks excellent English. Visitors will rarely find any difficulty in communicating with the people of Singapore.

Libraries and archives

Libraries

The National Library of Singapore in Stamford Road has a stock of more than 1·2 million titles – 158,000 in Malay, 355,000 in Chinese, 73,000 in Tamil and 647,000 in English.
It also possesses a large collection of microfilms, recordings and photographs and has a special section of books for the blind.

The National Library is open to the public (Mon.–Fri. 8.30 a.m.–8 p.m.).
The University Library System has more than 700,000 books, 6000 periodicals, 25,000 microfilm titles and an international selection of newspapers.

The National Archives, established in 1968, preserve documents on the history of Singapore dating back to 1805. The records are available for consultation by the public, except those less than 25 years old.
There is also a collection of microfilms of records in private hands.
The Ministry of Culture also runs an Oral History Unit, with recordings of personal accounts relating to the history of Singapore. Subjects already covered are the Singapore pioneers, the political development of Singapore between 1945 and 1965 and the Japanese occupation.

Archives

Lost property

Apply to Singapore Changi Airport.

Markets

See A to Z, Markets

Day markets

See A to Z

Night markets

Motoring

Singapore can be reached overland only by way of Malaysia. Since the international highway from Europe is interrupted in Burma, overland travellers from Europe via Asia must ship their vehicle from an Indian port.
A vehicle temporarily imported into Singapore for up to 12 months must be covered by a triptyque. Vehicles brought in for a shorter term, even from Malaysia, must have a carnet de passage.

Bringing your own car

Foreign drivers must have an international driving licence as well as their national licence.
Insurance of vehicles is compulsory in Singapore.

Documents

Traffic travels on the left, with overtaking on the right.
The speed limit within the city is 30 m.p.h. Singapore traffic is highly disciplined and is strictly controlled by the police.
Cars entering the Central Business District during the morning rush hour (7.30–10.15 Monday to Saturday) must purchase and display a Daily Area Licence, which costs 5 dollars.

Rule of the road

Breakdown service (24 hours a day): tel. 737 0831.
In the event of breakdown of a hired vehicle the car hire firm should be contacted.

Breakdown assistance

Information   Automobile Association of Singapore,
64 Lloyd Road, Singapore 0409
Tel. 737 2444 and 748 9911

Museums

In Singapore   National Museum
See A to Z, National Museum

On Sentosa Island   Art Centre
Coralarium
Maritime Museum
Shell Museum (Dari Laut)
Wax Museum
See A to Z, Sentosa Island

Admission to all these museums is free.

Music

See Folk traditions

Newspapers

All the major European newspapers are on sale in hotels and the larger newspaper kiosks; prices are high.
Singapore has Chinese, Malay and Tamil dailies, two English-language papers – the old-established "Straits Times" (morning) and the "Singapore Monitor" (afternoon) – and a business daily, the "Business Times". The "Straits Times" is noted for its full and excellent coverage of international news; local politics are handled with some caution, since an indirect form of censorship can be exercised through the requirement to obtain an annual publishing licence.

Night life

Discothèques   There are discothèques in most hotels. Information from the hotel reception or the Singapore Tourist Promotion Board.

Night clubs   Night clubs with a midnight floor-show and dancing are to be found in the large international hotels.

Cocktail lounges   In the cocktail lounges of hotels background music is often provided by a pianist, a guitar-player or a small orchestra.

Night markets   See A to Z

Chinese opera   See A to Z

Opening times

Usually open Mon.–Fri. 8 a.m.–5 p.m., Sat. 8 a.m.–1 p.m.   Public offices

Opening times vary, but are usually from 9.30 a.m. to 6 p.m.   Shops
Most shopping centres (see that entry, below) are open from
9.30 a.m. to 9 p.m.

Open Mon.–Fri. 10 a.m.–3 p.m., Sat. 9.30–11.30 a.m.   Banks

Open from 9 a.m.–5 p.m.   Museums

The best time is the early evening, but not between 7 and 8 p.m.   Private visits

Postal services

Singapore has 66 regular post offices providing all postal   Post offices
services and 56 branches providing more restricted facilities.
Urgent local mail posted in 24 post offices (indicated by special
signs) will be delivered to any part of the main island within $2\frac{1}{2}$
hours.

General Post Office,   Head post office
Fullerton Building, tel. 533 0234
Open 24 hours a day for telegrams and telephone service

Stamps can be bought in 66 post offices and from 131 licensed   Stamps
stamp-sellers.
For stamp-collectors there are two societies:
Singapore Philatelic Society, 160 Cross Street
Singapore Stamp Club, 28 Swattenham Road.

To Europe: Postage rates
letters (up to 10 grammes) 75 cents; postcards 40 cents
To the United States and Canada:
postcards 55 cents
To Australia and New Zealand:
postcards 25 cents
Aerogrammes to all parts of the world 35 cents

Singapore is linked up with the international telex network.   Telex
Telex is available at most hotels.

See that entry   Telephone services

Public transport

Public transport in Singapore is provided by buses.   Buses
The Singapore Bus Service has 2400 vehicles, running on 200
routes. In addition there is the CBD line 1 in the business
district.
The CSS Bus Service, running minibus shuttle services in the
central area, has 116 vehicles, on 9 routes.
The Blue Arrow Service has 16 buses on four express routes
serving the main island.

Practical Information

The Trans-Island Bus Services (TIBS) runs 194 buses on 12 routes in the districts of Sembawang and Woodlands. There is also an airport bus service, with four routes between the airport and all the larger hotels. Bus 390.

Timetables and maps

Detailed timetables and maps of the bus routes can be obtained from travel agencies, bookshops, stationers and newspaper kiosks.

Radio and television

Radio and television services are run by the State-controlled Singapore Broadcasting Corporation.
There are two television channels. Although some of the programmes are in Malay, Tamil and Mandarin, the majority are in English. This is also true of the radio programmes. In addition both the Malay television programmes can be received.

Rail travel

Malayan Railways (KTM) run daily train services between Singapore and all stations on the west coast of Malaysia, Kuala Lumpur, Penang/Butterworth and the northern part of the Malaysian east coast.
From Kuala Lumpur and Penang/Butterworth there are connections to Bangkok in Thailand.
The trains have 1st/2nd class compartments (some of them air-conditioned) and sleeping cars. 3rd class is not air-conditioned and has no sleepers.
Information tel: 222 5165.

Restaurants

A selection of well-known restaurants and their specialities:

Chinese

Cantonese food (balanced and delicately spiced) of excellent quality can be had in the following restaurants:

Union Farm Clementi Road, Eating House
Marinated chicken in foil

Hillman Restaurant,
Cantonment Road
Claypot dishes (meat, vegetables and seasonings simmered together)

Eastern Palace,
Supreme House, Penang Lane
Famous for its Cantonese banquets of up to 12 courses

Peking,
International Building

Mayfair,
DBS Building

Ming Palace,
Ming Court Hotel
Specialities: dim sum (morsels of pork, beef, poultry, seafood,
mushrooms and vegetables selected from a buffet)

Hokkien (famous for fish and seafood):
Food stalls in Hokkien Street, Rasa Singapura, Newton Circus
and, in Beng Hiang, in Food Alley on Murray Street

Teochew (Chinese fondue, also known as Mongolian hotpot):

Hung Kang Restaurant,
North Canal Road

Ban Seng Restaurant,
New Bridge Road
Specialties: grilled pork, baked duck

Chui Wah Lin,
Mosque Street
Speciality: Szechuan banquet

Hakka (giblets and other scraps, beautifully cooked):

Mei Kong Restaurant,
Murray Street

Szechuan specialties (substantial dishes, highly seasoned):

Apollo Hotel,
Havelock Road

Omei Restaurant,
Grand Central Hotel

Peking cuisine (the main speciality being Peking duck):

Eastern Palace,
Supreme House,

Shanghai Restaurant,
Mayfair Hotel
Speciality: birds-nest soup

Hot meat and vegetable curries

Omar Khayyam,
Hill Street
Mogul recipes, tandoori chicken

Banana Apollo Lear Restaurant,
Racecourse Road
South Asian cuisine

Moti Mahal,
Murray Street
North Indian and Kashmiri dishes

Practical Information

Ujahar Singh,
Gregory Place
Substantial meat dishes

Islamic Restaurant,
North Bridge Road

Gomez Curry,
Selegie House
Curries served on banana leaves

Komala Vilas,
Little India
Indian vegetarian cuisine

Indonesian

Indonesian cuisine is very similar to Malayan.

Rendezvous,
Bras Basah Road

Indonesian Restaurant,
Apollo Hotel

Jawa-Timor,
Market Street

Tambuah Mas,
Tanglin Shopping Centre

Japanese

Fujiya,
Shenton House

Okoh,
Supreme House

Kanako,
Goodwood Park Hotel

Yamagen,
Yen San Building, Orchard Road

Korean

Korean Restaurant,
Specialists' Centre, Orchard Road

Han Do,
Orchard Shopping Centre

Malayan

Highly spiced dishes, differing from Indian cuisine in their
particular mixtures of spices.

Food stalls in Newton Circus and Rasa Sayang Handicraft
Centre

Aziza Restaurant,
Emerald Hill Road

Satay Club,
Beach Road

In all the large international hotels   Western

See also Food and drink

Shopping centres

Singapore, the largest market centre for goods from all over the
world (particularly electronic and optical products from Asia),
has developed its attraction for tourists mainly through its
shopping centres. There are several dozen shopping centres
and shopping complexes, containing anything up to a hundred
or more individual shops. The total number of shops in
Singapore's shopping streets is beyond counting.
The range of products on display varies only slightly from
centre to centre. It is well worth while, therefore, to shop
around and compare prices so as to be able to bargain
effectively. It is also a good idea to know the prices of electronic
and optical products at home: Singapore prices are not always
necessarily lower.
All the shopping centres are air-conditioned, and most of them
also include banks and exchange offices, hairdressers and
beauty salons, travel agencies, airline offices, tailors' shops and
cafés.

The following is a selection of shopping centres:

Bukit Timah Plaza, Jalan Anak Bukit

Centre Point, Orchard Road

Change Alley Aerial Plaza, Collyer Quay

Changi Village Shopping Complex, Changi Village

Colombo Court, North Bridge Road

Cuppage Road Shopping Centre

Far East Shopping Centre, Orchard Road

The Gallery, Battery Road

Golden Mile Shopping Centre, Beach Road

High Street Centre, North Bridge Road

Katong Shopping Centre, Mountbatten Road

Lucky Plaza, Orchard Road

Orchard Shopping Centre, Orchard Road

Orchard Towers, Orchard Road

Outram Park Shopping Centre, Outram Road

Peace Centre, Sophia Road

Pearl's Centre, Eu Tong Sen Street

Peninsula Shopping Centre, Coleman Street

People's Park Centre, New Bridge Road

People's Park Complex, New Bridge Road

Plaza Singapura, Orchard Road

The Promenade, Orchard Road

Specialists' Centre, Orchard Road

Supreme House, Penang Road

Tanglin Shopping Centre, Tanglin Road

The Orchard, Orchard Road

There are other shopping centres listed in the telephone directory – yellow pages.

See also Department stores and Specialist shops

Sightseeing tours

Coach tours	Singapore's travel agencies offer a variety of coach tours of the city and the island. Information from hotels, travel agencies and the Tourist Promotion Board.
Special tours	The travel agents of Singapore organise tours catering for particular interests. On these tours the commentary is in English and in other international languages. The most popular tours are: Trishaw (bicycle-rickshaw); in the footsteps of Raffles; city tour; Sentosa Island; a walk in the jungle; Jurong Bird Park; the east coast; the zoo; guided tour of the cuisine of Singapore (hawker stalls); guided tour through rubber plantations; excursion to Malacca (Johore). Participants are normally collected from their hotel. All tours can be arranged and booked on an individual basis.
Individual tours	Guides for individual tours can be obtained through the Tourist Promotion Board.
Boat trips	See that entry

Souvenirs

Although Singapore produces no genuine souvenirs of its own it ranks with Hong Kong as the largest market in Asia for the sale of antiques, craft products and curios from all over the world, particularly from Asia.
See Antiques, Department stores, Shopping centres, Specialist shops

Specialist shops

Select Books, Tanglin Shopping Centre, Tanglin Road,   Books
tel. 737 8295
MPH, Malaysian Publishing House, Robinson Road

Amir and Sons, Lucky Plaza, tel. 737 3355   Carpets
Oriental Carpet Palace, 163 H, Singapore Handicraft Centre,
Tanglin Road, tel. 235 8259
Hassan's Carpets, 177 Orchard Road, tel. 737 5626

Chen Yee Shen, Orchard Towers, Orchard Road, tel. 737 1174   Chinese arts and crafts
Funan Art, Tanglin Shopping Centre, tel. 737 3442
Beijing Antiques, Far East Plaza, Scotts Road, tel. 734 7878
Ming Village, Pandan Road, tel. 265 7711
Peiping Store, Handicraft Centre, tel. 235 9058
Paul Art Gallery, Supreme House, Penang Road, tel. 338 1217

Golden Million Coin & Currency Agency, 11 Collyer Quay,   Coins
tel. 223 1044

Centrepoint Complex, Mayfair Reptiles, Orchard Road,   Crocodile-skin and leather
tel. 235 0931   goods
Far East Plaza, Scotts Road; several dealers
Far East Shopping Centre, Orchard Road, Les Must De Cartier,
tel. 235 3158
Gold Hill Square, Gilbarto/Colnago, tel. 256 8116
Lucky Plaza, Orchard Road; several dealers
Plaza Singapura, Orchard Road; several dealers

Katong Flower Shop, LG 12, Lower Ground Floor; Orchard   Flowers
Plaza, Orchard Road, tel. 235 0840

Lee Onn, 206–208 South Bridge Road, tel. 223 5533   Jewellery
Eramanis, G 14, Ground Floor, Tanglin Shopping Centre,
Tanglin Road, tel. 737 3246
Kampooli, G 7, Ground Floor, Plaza Singapura, Orchard Road,
tel. 336 1381
C. T. Hoo, 27 Tanglin Road, tel. 235 9343
Jewellery, Park Hotel
Tin Sing Goldsmiths, 215–217 South Bridge Road,
tel. 223 4150

Handloom House, 3–14 Orchard Towers, tel. 235 1542   Silk
Chinese silk:
China Silk House, 111–113, First Floor, Tanglin Shopping
Centre, Tanglin Road, tel. 235 5020

De Silva, Tanglin Shopping Centre, Tanglin Road,   Silver
tel. 737 8528

Tien Kee Brothers (Bali House), 23–27 Middle Road,   Souvenirs and Gifts
tel. 338 1803
Singapore Woodcraft, 318 Third Floor, Plaza Singapura,
Orchard Road, tel. 337 7777
Singapore Souvenirs, B1–10 Lucky Plaza, Orchard Road,
tel. 737 2886

Made to measure: a tailor's shop in Singapore

Seah Gallery, M 5 Mezzanine Floor, Shangri-La, tel. 235 0923
Loong Souvenirs, 2-107 Far East Plaza, Scotts Road,
tel. 733 3903

Tailors

Fashion Tailors, 245 Orchard Road, tel. 737 4043
Heero's Custom Tailors, G 50 Lucky Plaza, Orchard Road,
tel. 235 3225
Shanghai Ladies' Dressmaker, 4–63 Lucky Plaza,
tel. 235 2002
Tat Bee Tailors, Lucky Plaza, tel. 235 3366
Steven Bespoke Tailor, 11 Collyer Quay, The Arcade,
tel. 222 7136
Fatman, 2–27 Centrepoint, Orchard Road, tel. 737 9472

Sport

The National Stadium, managed by the Singapore Sports
Council, can accommodate 60,000 spectators. Associated
with it are facilities for athletics, squash, tennis, and golf and a
gymnasium. The Council also administers 6 athletic centres, 34
multi-purpose playing fields and pitches, 3 indoor stadiums, 17
swimming complexes, 16 netball courts, 51 tennis courts, 28
squash courts and several fitness centres.
The following are some of the principal sports clubs and
facilities:

Badminton

Badminton Hall, Guillemard Road, tel. 245 1222

Changi Sailing Club, Netheravon Road, tel. 445 1298
Singapore Armed Forces Yacht Club, Seletar Air Base,
tel. 481 0184
Ponggol Boatel, tel. 280 6444
Republic of Singapore Yacht Club, Jalan Buroh, tel. 265 0931

Boating

Bowling Centre, Hyatt Singapore Hotel, tel. 737 5511
Jackie's Bowl, 542-B East Coast Road, tel. 241 6519
Jackie's Bowl, 8 Grange Road, tel. 737 4744
Jurong Family Bowl, Yuan Ching Road, tel. 265 5433
Kallang Bowl, 5 Stadium Walk, tel. 345 0545
Pasir Panjang Bowl, Pasir Panjang Road, tel. 775 5555
Plaza Bowl, 3rd floor, Textile Centre, Jalan Sultan,
tel. 292 4821
Starbowl, 5th floor, Peace Centre, tel. 338 1421

Bowling

Republic of Singapore Flying Club, East Camp, tel. 481 0502

Flying

Changi Golf Club, Netheravon Road, tel. 445 1298
Jurong Country Club, Jurong Town Hall Road, tel. 265 5655
Sembawang Golf Club, Sembawang Road, tel. 257 4714
Singapore Island Country Club, Upper Thomson Road,
tel. 453 1222
Tanglin Golf Course, Minden Road, tel. 63 7236
Sentosa Golf Club, Sentosa Island, tel. 62 2722

Golf

National Stadium Gymnasium, Kallang, tel. 345 1222

Gymnastics

Singapore Turf Club, Bukit Timah Road, tel. 468 3366 (see
A to Z – Turf Club)

Horse-racing

Singapore Squash Centre, Fort Canning Rise, tel. 337 4280
Farrer Park, Rutland Road, tel. 293 1664
Changi Squash Courts, Cranwell Road, tel. 445 2941
National Stadium, Kallang, tel. 345 1222

Squash

Alexandra Park, Royal Road, tel. 63 7236
Changi Tennis Court, Cranwell Road, tel. 445 2941
Farrer Park, Rutland Road, tel. 293 1664

Tennis

Singapore Sub-Aqua Club, tel. 445 6253

Underwater sports

Ponggol Boatel, Ponggol Point, tel. 280 6444

Water-skiing

Taxis

Singapore has more than 11,000 taxis, over 8000 of them air-
conditioned. All have meters, which the driver is obliged by law
to switch on.
Taxis can be picked up at taxi ranks, hailed in the street or called
by telephone (tel. 452 5555, 293 3111 or 250 0700: 24 hours
a day service).

The starting fare is 2 dollars (2·20 dollars for air-conditioned
taxis) for the first 1500 metres or part thereof, plus 20 cents

Fares

for every subsequent 500 metres (over 10 km 40 cents per 500 m) and 10 cents for every minute of waiting time or part thereof.

For taxis called by telephone there is an additional charge of 1 dollar, but the meter is not turned on until the passenger boards the taxi.

There is a surcharge of 1 dollar for journeys starting in the Central Business District between 4 and 7 p.m. on weekdays and 12 noon and 3 p.m. on Saturdays. Taxis entering the Central Business District must have a Daily Area Licence, the fee for which (5 dollars) is payable either by the driver or the passenger.

Telegrams

Telegrams, both local and international, can be sent by telephone, at either normal or urgent rates, in English or other languages.

Telephone services

Singapore's telephone service is of the most modern technical standard, and is linked with the international telephone network by submarine cable and satellite. International calls are rapid and clear.

Direct dialling

Dialling codes:
United Kingdom to Singapore: 010 65
United States or Canada to Singapore: 011 65
Singapore to United Kingdom; 005 44
Singapore to United States or Canada: 005 1

Tariffs

Local calls from pay-phones cost 10 cents; from private telephones they are free.
Emergency calls (999 and 995) are free, except from pay-phones.

Information

Dial 103

Telex

Telex messages can be handed in at Telecoms Building, 35 Robinson Road.

Television

See Radio and television

Time

Singapore Standard Time is 8 hours ahead of Greenwich Mean Time.

Tipping

Most hotels and restaurants add a service charge to the bill.
Tipping is expressly discouraged.
The Tourist Promotion Board is waging a campaign against
tipping. Visitors who want to show appreciation for some
particular service should not give more than 50 cents or 2
dollars according to the service rendered.

Toilets

Toilets in Singapore are up to European standards. All
shopping centres are adequately provided with public toilets.

Tourist information

See Information

Travel agencies

Singapore has 319 registered travel agencies. All agencies
must be licensed by the government.
A list of travel agents can be found in the yellow pages of the
telephone directory.
Most agencies deal with both domestic and international
travel.
There is fierce competition in the tourist trade, and it is,
therefore, well worth while shopping around and comparing
prices.
Complaints about the service provided by a travel agency
should be addressed to the Singapore Tourist Promotion
Board.

Travel documents

All persons entering Singapore must have a valid passport or
other internationally recognised travel document. Visas are not
required for British subjects or Commonwealth citizens, or for
United States citizens entering Singapore in transit or for a
temporary stay for any purpose other than employment or
residence.

Passport

A smallpox vaccination certificate is not required, except for
visitors who within the preceding 14 days have been in an area
where there is smallpox. Similarly, a yellow fever vaccination
certificate is required only for visitors who within the preceding
6 days have passed through a country in which yellow fever is
either partly or wholly endemic. A cholera vaccination
certificate is not now required.

Health requirements

Singapore Immigration Department, Empress Place,
tel. 337 4031
Open Mon.–Fri. 8 a.m.–5 p.m., Sat. 8 a.m.–1 p.m.

Immigration authorities

Tropical parks and nature reserves

Singapore, an island state with no hinterland to speak of, has made great efforts to conserve as much open space as possible, both in the city itself and in the rest of the island. Its image as a garden city concerned to preserve its tropical flora and fauna is thoroughly well earned.

The city has many parks and gardens, with footpaths winding their way amid tropical plants and a colourful sea of flowers. Outside the city some areas of natural jungle have been preserved intact, under statutory protection.

The following are the best known parks and gardens:

Central Park
See A to Z

Elizabeth Walk
See A to Z

Empress Place
See A to Z

Jurong
See A to Z, Jurong Town

MacRitchie Reservoir
See A to Z

Mount Faber
See A to Z

Padang
See A to Z

Seletar Reservoir
See A to Z

Sentosa Island
See A to Z

Mandai Orchid Garden
See A to Z

Botanic Gardens
See A to Z

Bukit Timah Nature Reserve
See A to Z

Weather forecast

Weather forecasts are included in the television news bulletins and published in the daily papers. Tide tables: apply to the Tourist Promotion Board.

Weather conditions for shipping: see the daily Press or apply to the Port of Singapore Authority, tel. 271 2211.

Weights and measures

Singapore is on the metric system.

When to go to Singapore

The best time to visit Singapore is outside the monsoon season
– i.e. from the end of March to June. Weather conditions are
also very pleasant, however, during the north-east monsoon
(December to March) and the south-west monsoon (June to
September). Rain falls for only a few hours each day, after
which the sky becomes cloudless again.
Singapore lies only 100 km (60 miles) from the Equator.
Average day temperatures are about 30 °C (86 °F), and night
temperatures are only slightly lower.

Useful Telephone Numbers

Emergencies
  Police   999
  Fire, ambulance, doctor   995
  Breakdown assistance   748 9911

Information
  Singapore Tourist Promotion Board   235 6611
  Airport   542 5680
  Rail bookings   222 5165
  Immigration Department   337 4031
  Automobile Association of Singapore   737 2444

Diplomatic missions
  United Kingdom   63 9333
  United States   338 0251
  Canada   737 1322
  Australia   737 9311
  New Zealand   235 9966

Airlines
  British Airways   253 8444
  PanAm   220 0711
  Singapore Airlines   223 8888

Singapore General Hospital   222 3322

Taxis   452 5555, 293 3111, 250 0700

Telegrams   533 0234

Telephones
  Calls to United Kingdom   005 44
  Calls to USA or Canada   005 1
  Information – international calls   162
  Information – local calls   103